A Doctrine and Life Special

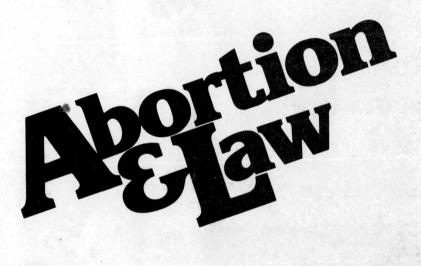

First published (1983) by
Dominican Publications
St Saviour's
Dublin 1

ISBN 0 907271 19 7

© Dominican Publications

Cover design by Edward McManus

Typeset and printed by
The Leinster Leader Ltd.
Naas
Co. Kildare

Contents

About this Book

AUSTIN FLANNERY, O.P.

This book owes its origin to the public debate, still current at the time of going to press, on the proposal to add to the Irish Constitution an amendment designed to protect the life of the unborn. It had been intended to publish the book earlier, but this was not possible. In the event, the delay proved fortunate, enabling us to take account of the actual amendment which, as now seems very likely, is to be put to a referendum.

The bulk of the contributions, however, were written before the proposed wording was known and when it was widely assumed that a different approach would be adopted, one involving the prohibition of abortion, rather than the assertion of the rights of the unborn. Thus, three of the contributors, Fathers Brendan O'Mahony, O.F.M.Cap., Bernard Treacy, O.P. and Conleth A. Byrne, O.P., discuss the difficulties and the legal and social implications of an amendment which would prohibit abortion, either absolutely or with one or more exceptions. All three are totally opposed to abortion. For them, as indeed for the other contributors, the only matter open to discussion is the advisability and feasibility of a constitutional amendment on the matter.

Mr William Binchy, whose contribution was written later, addresses himself directly to the amendment which is now proposed, as do Fathers Treacy and Byrne in additional contributions.

The Catholic Church in Ireland has made no official pronouncement on the proposed amendment, but the Church's teaching on abortion is a crucial ingredient in the entire debate. For this reason, we have reproduced in full three important documents on the subject — by the Sacred Congregation for the Doctrine of the Faith, the Bishops of Ireland and the Archbishops of Britain.

The main focus of the book, however, is on the issues which surfaced during the debate, issues such as pluralism, the nature and function of a constitution, the relation between morality and law, sectarianism, secularism.

Thus Fathers O'Mahony, Byrne and Treacy treat of these matters in their contributions, with Father Byrne taking issue with Father O'Mahony on a number of points. Father Fergal O'Connor and Dr Garrett Barden tease out in greater detail the meanings of pluralism and the role of interest groups and of the legislature in a democracy.

Mrs Jane Linden and the pseudonymous Mrs Anne Smith

marshall their own arguments against abortion.

When the dust will have settled after the current debate on the proposed amendment, much will need to be done, over a long period of time, whatever the outcome. Women who will have had abortions and will have subsequently been driven to near despair with remorse will continue to need pastoral care. Pregnant single women who opt for parenthood rather than abortion will continue to need help of the kind so magnificently provided by organizations such as ALLY. There will be an on-going need for the amelioration of the social attitudes and of the economic factors which to the agonized mind of a pregnant single girl can make abortion preferable to parenthood. The legal stigma of illegitimacy must be removed, as Mr Binchey says in his article. There will now be greater need than ever for clear teaching on the evil of abortion, which is why we include the articles by Mrs Linden and Mrs Smith and the three official church documents.

Fathers Byrne and Treacy doubt that the proposed amendment will be fully effective if voted into our constitution. While it would make it impossible for a Court or for the Oireachtas to assert that an unborn child has no rights, as has been stated in the United States, there is nothing in it, Father Treacy believes, 'which would prevent a Court or the Oireachtas from providing for the resolution . . .' of 'conflicts arising between the rights of the mother and child'.

Father Byrne says of the proposed amendment that it 'attempts to avoid being divisive' and, doubtless, this was very much in the mind of those who framed it. However, it is clear from several statements in the press that some other Christian Churches do see it as divisive. This is something which needs to be faced honestly and sympathetically by our legislators.

NOTE

As this book was going to press, the Bill to provide an amendment to the Irish Constitution, protecting the right to life of the unborn, was being debated in the Dáil. On 9 February 1983 the minister responsible for guiding the Bill through its parliamentary stages, the Minister for Justice, stated that in approving of the principle of the Bill deputies would not, as far as he was concerned, be committing themselves to the particular wording now proposed or any other particular form of wording, but only to the principle.

Declaration on Procured Abortion*

SACRED CONGREGATION FOR THE DOCTRINE OF THE FAITH

(I) INTRODUCTION

(1) The problem of procured abortion and of its possible legal liberalization has become almost everywhere the subject of im-passioned discussions. These debates would be less important were it not a question of human life, a primordial value, which must be protected and promoted. Everyone understands this, although many argue, even against all the evidence, for increased recourse to abortion. One cannot but be astonished to see an increase of unqualified protests against the death penalty and every form of war and simultaneously the vindication of the liberalization of abortion, either on demand or with – progressively diminishing – restrictions. The Church is too conscious of the fact that it belongs to her vocation to defend man against everything that could destroy or diminish his dignity to remain silent on such a topic. Because the Son of God became man, there is no man who is not his brother in humanity and who is not called to become a Christian in order to receive salvation from him.

(2) In many countries the public authorities which resist the liberalization of abortion laws are the object of powerful pressures aimed at leading them to this goal. This, it is said, would violate no one's conscience, for each individual would be left free to follow his own opinion, while being prevented from imposing it on others. Ethical pluralism is claimed to be a normal consequence of ideolo-gical pluralism. There is, however, a great difference between the one and the other, for action affects the interests of others more quickly than does mere opinion. Moreover, one can never claim freedom of opinion as a pretext for attacking the rights of others, most especially the right to life.

(3) Numerous Christian lay people, especially doctors, but also parents' associations, statesmen, or leading figures in posts of responsibility have vigorously reacted against this propaganda campaign. Above all, many episcopal conferences and many bishops acting in their own name have judged it opportune to recall very

*This is an 'official', but in parts quite defective, translation. Where necessary we have corrected it from the Latin original published in the *Osservatore Romano*, 25-26 November 1974. (Editor,' DOCTRINE AND LIFE.)

strongly the traditional doctrine of the Church.[1] With a striking convergence these documents admirably emphasize an attitude of respect for life which is at the same time human and Christian. Nevertheless, it has happened that several of these documents have not been fully accepted or have been rejected.

(4) Charged with the promotion and the defence of faith and morals in the universal Church,[2] the Sacred Congregation for the Doctrine of the Faith proposes to recall this teaching in its essential aspects to all the faithful. Thus, in showing the unity of the Church, it will confirm by the authority proper to the Holy See what the bishops have opportunely undertaken. It hopes that all the faithful, including those who might have been unsettled by the controversies and new opinions, will understand that it is not a question of opposing one opinion to another, but of transmitting to the faithful a constant teaching of the supreme magisterium, which teaches moral principles in the light of faith.[3] It is therefore clear that this declaration necessarily entails a grave obligation for Christian consciences.[4] May God deign to enlighten also all men who strive with their whole heart to 'act in truth' (John 3:21).

(II) IN THE LIGHT OF FAITH

(5) 'Death was not God's doing, he takes no pleasure in the extinction of the living' (Wis. 1:13). Certainly God has created beings who have only one lifetime and physical death cannot be absent from the world of those with a bodily existence. But what is immediately willed is life, and in the visible universe everything has been made for man, who is the image of God and the world's crowning glory (cf. Gen. 1:26-28). On the human level, 'it was the devil's envy that brought death into the world' (Wis. 2:24). Introduced by sin, death remains bound up with it : death is the sign and

1. A certain number of bishops' documents are to be found in Gr. Caprile, *Non Uccidere. Il Magistero della Chiesa sull'aborto,* par. II, pp. 47-300, Rome, 1973.

2. *Regimini Ecclesiae Universae,* III, 1, 29. Cf. *ibid.,* 31 (*AAS* 59 (1967), p. 897). On the Sacred Congregation for the Doctrine of the Faith depend all the questions which are related to faith and morals or which are bound up with the faith.

3. *Lumen Gentium,* 12 (*AAS* 57 (1965), pp. 16-17). The present Declaration does not envisage all the questions which can arise in connection with abortion : it is for theologians to examine and discuss them. Only certain basic principles are here recalled which must be for the theologians themselves a guide and a rule, and confirm certain fundamental truths of Catholic doctrine for all Christians.

4. *Lumen Gentium,* 25 (*AAS* 57 (1965), pp. 29-31).

fruit of sin. But there is no final triumph for death. Confirming faith in the resurrection, the Lord proclaims in the gospel : 'God is God, not of the dead, but of the living' (Mt. 22:32). And death like sin will be definitively defeated by resurrection in Christ (cf. 1 Cor. 15:20-27). Thus we understand that human life, even on this earth, is precious. Infused by the creator,[5] life is again taken back by him (cf. Gen. 2:7; Wis. 15:11). It remains under his protection : man's blood cries out to him (cf. Gen. 4:10) and he will demand an account of it, 'for in the image of God man was made' (Gen. 9:5-6). The commandment of God is formal : 'You shall not kill' (Ex. 20:13). Life is at the same time a gift and a responsibility. It is received as a 'talent' (cf. Mt. 25:14-30); it must be put to proper use. In order that life may bring forth fruit, many tasks are offered to man in this world and he must not shirk them. More important still, the Christian knows that eternal life depends on what, with the grace of God, he does with his life on earth.

(6) The tradition of the Church has always held that human life must be protected and cherished from the beginning, just as at the various stages of its development. Opposing the morals of the Greco-Roman world, the Church of the first centuries insisted on the difference that exists on this point between those morals and Christian morals. In the *Didaché* it is clearly said : 'You shall not kill by abortion the fruit of the womb and you shall not murder the infant already born.'[6] Athenagoras emphasizes that Christians consider as murderers those women who take medicines to procure an abortion; he condemns the killers of children, including those still living in their mother's womb, 'where they are already the object of the care of divine providence'.[7] Tertullian did not always perhaps use the same language; he nevertheless clearly affirms the

---

5. The authors of Scripture do not make any philosophical observations on when life begins but they speak of the period of life which precedes birth as being the object of God's attention : he creates and forms the human being, like that which is moulded by his hand (cf. Ps. 118 : 73). It would seem that this theme finds expression for the first time in Jr. 1 : 5. It appears later in many other texts. Cf. Is. 49 : 1, 5; 46 : 3; Jb. 10 : 8-12, Ps. 22 : 10, 71 : 6, 139 : 13. In the Gospels we read in Luke 1 : 44 : 'For the moment your greeting reached my ears, the child in my womb leapt for joy.'

6. *Didaché Apostolorum,* edition Funk, *Patres Apostolici,* V, 2. *The Epistle of Barnabas,* XIX, 5, uses the same expressions (cf. Funk, *l.c.,* 91-93).

7. Athenagoras, *A Plea on behalf of Christians,* 35 (cf. *PG* 6,970 : *S.C.* 3, pp. 166-167). One may also consult the *Epistle to Diognetus,* V, 6 Funk, *o.c.,* 1,399 : *S.C.* 33), where it says of Christians : 'They procreate children, but they do not reject the foetus'.

essential principle : 'To prevent birth is anticipated murder; it makes little difference whether one destroys a life already born or does away with it in its nascent stage. The one who will be a man is already one.'[8]

(7) In the course of history, the Fathers of the Church, her Pastors and her Doctors have taught the same doctrine – the various opinions on the infusion of the spiritual soul did not cast doubt on the illicitness of abortion. It is true that in the Middle Ages, when the opinion was generally held that the spiritual soul was not present until after the first few weeks, a distinction was made in the evaluation of the sin and the gravity of penal sanctions. In resolving cases, approved authors were more lenient with regard to that early stage than with regard to later stages. But it was never denied at that time that procured abortion, even during the first days, was objectively a grave sin. This condemnation was in fact unanimous. It is enough to cite some from among the many documents. The First Council of Mainz in 847 reconsiders the penalties against abortion which had been established by preceding Councils. It decided that the most rigorous penance would be imposed 'on women who procure the elimination of the fruit conceived in their womb'.[9] The Decree of Gratian reports the following words of Pope Stephen V : 'That person is a murderer who causes to perish by abortion what has been conceived.'[10] St Thomas, the Common Doctor of the Church, teaches that abortion is a grave sin against the natural law.[11] At the time of the Renaissance Pope Sixtus V condemned abor-

---

8. Tertullian, *Apologeticum,* IX, 8 *PL* 1,371-372 : *Corp. Christ.* I, p. 103, 1.31-36).

9. Canon 21 (Mansi, 14, p. 909). Cf. Council of Elvira, canon 63 (Mansi, 2, p. 16) and the Council of Ancyra, canon 21 (*ibid.,* 519). See also the decree of Gregory III regarding the penance to be imposed upon those who are guilty of this crime (Mansi 13,292, c. 17).

10. Gratian, *Concordantia Discordantium Canonum,* c. 20, C. 2, q. 2. During the Middle Ages appeal was often made to the authority of Saint Augustine who wrote as follows in regard to this matter in *De Nuptiis et Concupiscentiis,* c. 15 : 'Sometimes this sexually indulgent cruelty or this cruel sexual indulgence goes so far as to procure potions which produce sterility. If the desired result is not achieved, the mother terminates the life and expels the foetus which was in her womb in such a way that the child dies before having lived or, if the baby was living already in its mother's womb, it is killed before being born' (*PL* 44,423-424 : CSEL 33, 619. Cf. the *Decree of Gratian,* q. 2, C 32, c. 7).

11. *Commentary on the Sentences,* book IV, dist. 31, exposition of the text.

tion with the greatest severity.[12] A century later, Innocent XI rejected the propositions of certain lax canonists who sought to excuse an abortion procured before the moment accepted by some as the moment of the spiritual animation of the new being.[13] In our days the recent Roman Pontiffs have proclaimed the same doctrine with the greatest clarity. Pius XI explicitly answered the most serious objections.[14] Pius XII clearly excluded all direct abortion, that is, abortion which is either an end or a means.[15] John XXIII recalled the teaching of the Fathers on the sacred character of life 'which from its beginning demands the action of God the creator'.[16] Most recently, the Second Vatican Council, presided over by Paul VI, has most severely condemned abortion : 'Life must be safeguarded with extreme care from conception; abortion and infanticide are abominable crimes.'[17] The same Paul VI, speaking on this subject on many occasions, has not hesitated to declare that this teaching of the Church 'has not changed and is unchangeable'.[18]

(III) IN THE ADDITIONAL LIGHT OF REASON

(8) Respect for human life is not just a Christian obligation. Human reason is sufficient to impose it on the basis of the analysis of what a human person is and should be. Constituted by

12. Constitutio *Effraenatum* in 1588 (*Bullarium Romanum,* V, 1, pp. 25-27; *Fontes Iuris Canonici,* I, no. 165, pp. 308-311).
13. Dz-Sch 1184. Cf. also the Constitution *Apostolicae Sedis* of Pius IX (Acta Pii IX, V, 55-72; *ASS* 5 (1869), pp. 305-331; *Fontes Iuris Canonici,* III, no. 552, pp. 24-31).
14. Encyclical *Casti Connubii, AAS* 22 (1930), pp. 562-565; Dz-Sch. 3719-21.
15. The statements of Pius XII are express, precise and numerous; they would require a whole study on their own. We quote only this one from the Discourse to the Saint Luke Union of Italian Doctors of 12 November 1944, because it formulates the principle in all its universality: 'As long as a man is not guilty, his life is untouchable, and therefore any act directly tending to destroy it is illicit, whether such destruction is intended as an end in itself or only as a means to an end, whether it is a question of life in the embryonic stage or in a stage of full development or already in its final stages' (Discourses and Radio-messages, VI, 183ff.).
16. Encyclical *Mater et Magistra, AAS* 53 (1961), p. 447.
17. *Gaudium et Spes,* 51. Cf. 27 (*AAS* 58 (1966), p. 1072; cf. 1047).
18. The Speech: *Salutiamo con paterna effusione,* 9 December 1972, *AAS* 64 (1972), p. 737. Among the witnesses of this unchangeable doctrine one will recall the declaration of the Holy Office, condemning direct abortion (Denzinger 1890, *ASS* 17 (1884), p. 556; 22 (1888-1890), 748; Dz-Sch 3258).

a rational nature, man is a person, a subject capable of reflecting on himself and of determining his acts and hence his own destiny : he is free. He is consequently master of himself, or rather, because self-mastery takes time, he has the means of becoming so : this is his task. Created immediately by God, man's soul is spiritual and therefore immortal. Hence man is open to God; he finds his fulfilment only in him. But he spends his life in the company of his own kind. He is nourished, as it were, by interpersonal relationships in society. And society is indispensable to him. While society and other men must be taken into account, each human person possesses himself, he possesses life and goods; he has these as a right. It is this that strict justice demands from all in his regard.

(9) Nevertheless, temporal life lived in this world does not exhaust all that pertains to the person, for he has a higher and indeed everlasting life of his own. Bodily life is a fundamental good; here below it is the condition for all other goods. But there are higher values for which it could be legitimate or even necessary to be willing to expose oneself to the risk of losing bodily life. In a society of persons the common good is for each individual an end which he must serve and to which he must subordinate his particular interest. But it is not his last end and, from this point of view, it is society which is at the service of the person, because the person will not fulfil his destiny except in God. The person can be definitively subordinated only to God. Man can never be treated simply as a means to be disposed of in order to obtain a higher end.

(10) In regard to the mutual rights and duties of the person and of society, it belongs to moral teaching to enlighten consciences, it belongs to the law to specify and organize external behaviour. There is a definite number of rights which society is not in a position to grant since these rights precede society; but it is society's function to preserve and to enforce them. These comprise most of what today we call 'human rights' and which our age boasts of having formulated.

(11) The first right of the human person is his life. He has other goods and some are more precious, but this one is fundamental – the condition of all the others. It does not belong to society, nor does it belong to public authority in any form to recognize this right for some and not for others : all discrimination is evil, whether it be founded on race, sex, colour or religion. It is not recognition by another that constitutes this right. This right is antecedent to its recognition; it demands recognition and it is strictly unjust to refuse it.

(12) Any discrimination based on the various stages of life is no more justified than any other discrimination. The right to life remains complete in an old person, even one greatly weakened, it is not lost by one who is incurably sick. The right to life is no less to be respected in the small infant just born than in the mature person. In reality, respect for human life is called for from the time that the process of generation begins. From the time that the ovum is fertilized, a life is begun which is neither that of the father nor of the mother; it is rather the life of a new human being with his own growth. It would never be made human if it were not human already.

(13) This has always been clear, and discussions about the moment of animation have no bearing on it.[19] Modern genetic science offers clear confirmation. It has demonstrated that, from the first instant there is established the programme of what this living being will be : a man, this individual man with his characteristic aspects already well determined. Right from fertilization the adventure of a human life begins, and each of its capacities requires time – a rather lengthy time – to find its place and to be in a position to act. The least that can be said is that present science, in its most evolved state, does not give any substantial support to those who defend abortion. Moreover, it is not up to biological sciences to make a definitive judgment on questions which are properly philosophical and moral, such as the moment when a human person is constituted or the legitimacy of abortion. From a moral point of view this is certain : even if a doubt existed concerning whether the fruit of conception is already a human person, it is objectively a grave sin to dare to risk murder. 'The one who will be a man is already one.'[20]

---

19. This declaration expressly leaves aside the question of the moment when the spiritual soul is infused. There is not a unanimous tradition on this point and authors are as yet in disagreement. For some it dates from the first instant, for others it could not at least precede nidation. It is not within the competence of science to decide between these views, because the existence of an immortal soul is not a question in its field. It is a philosophical problem from which our moral affirmation remains independent for two reasons : (i) supposing a later animation, there is still nothing less than a *human* life, preparing for and calling for a soul in which the nature received from parents is completed; (2) on the other hand it suffices that this presence of the soul be probable (and one can never prove the contrary) in order that the taking of life involve accepting the risk of killing a man, not only waiting for, but already in possession of his soul.

20. Tertullian, cited in footnote 8.

(IV) REPLY TO SOME OBJECTIONS

(14) Divine law and natural reason, therefore, exclude all right to the direct killing of an innocent man. However, if the reasons given to justify an abortion were always manifestly evil and valueless the problem would not be so dramatic. The gravity of the problem comes from the fact that in certain cases, perhaps in quite a considerable number of cases, by denying abortion one endangers important values which men normally hold in great esteem and which may sometimes even seem to have priority. We do not deny these very great difficulties. It may be a serious question of health, sometimes of life or death, for the mother; it may be the burden represented by an additional child, especially if there are good reasons to fear that the child will be abnormal or retarded; it may be the importance attributed in different classes of society to considerations of honour or dishonour, of loss of social standing, and so forth. We proclaim only that none of these reasons can ever objectively confer the right to dispose of another's life, even when that life is only beginning. With regard to the future unhappiness of the child, no one, not even the father or mother, can act as its substitute, even if it is still in the embryonic stage, to choose in the child's name, life or death. The child itself, when grown up, will never have the right to choose suicide; no more may his parents choose death for the child while it is not of an age to decide for itself. Life is too fundamental a value to be weighed against even very serious disadvantages.[21]

(15) The movement for the emancipation of women, in so far as it seeks essentially to free them from all unjust discrimination, is perfectly justified.[22] In many areas of society much remains to be done in this respect. But one cannot change nature. Nor can one exempt women, any more than men, from what nature demands of them. Furthermore, all publicly recognized freedom is always limited by the certain rights of others.

(16) The same must be said of the claim to sexual freedom. If by this expression one is to understand the mastery progressively acquired by reason and by authentic love over instinctive impulse,

21. See Cardinal Villot, Secretary of State, on 10 October 1973 to Cardinal Döpfner, regarding the protection of human life (*L'Osservatore Romano*, German edition, 26 October 1973, p. 3).
22. Encyclical *Pacem in Terris, AAS* 55 (1963), p. 267. Constitution *Gaudium et Spes*, 29. Speech of Paul VI, *Salutiamo, AAS* 64 (1972), 779.

without diminishing pleasure but keeping it in its proper place -- and in this sphere this is the only authentic freedom – then there is nothing to object to. But this kind of freedom will always be careful not to violate justice. If, on the contrary, one is to understand that men and women are 'free' to seek sexual pleasure to the point of satiety, without taking into account any law or the essential orientation of sexual life towards fertility,[23] then this idea has nothing Christian in it. It is even unworthy of man. In any case it does not confer any right to dispose of human life – even if embryonic – or to suppress it on the pretext that it is burdensome.

(17) Scientific progress is opening to technology – and will open still more – the possibility of delicate interventions, the consequences of which can be very serious, for good as well as for evil. These are achievements of the human spirit which in themselves are admirable. But technology can never be independent of the criterion of morality, since technology exists for man and must respect his finality. Just as there is no right to use nuclear energy for every possible purpose, so there is no right to manipulate human life in every possible direction. Technology must be at the service of man, so as better to ensure the functioning of his normal abilities, to prevent or to cure his illnesses, to contribute to his better human development. It is true that the evolution of technology makes early abortion more and more easy, but the moral evaluation is in no way modified because of this.

(18) We know what seriousness the problem of birth control can assume for some families and for some countries. That is why the last Council and subsequently the Encyclical *Humanae Vitae* of 25 July 1968, spoke of 'responsible parenthood'.[24] What we wish to say again with emphasis, as was pointed out in the conciliar Constitution *Gaudium et Spes,* in the Encyclical *Populorum Progressio* and in other papal documents, is that never, under any pretext, may abortion be resorted to, either by a family or by the political authority, as a legitimate means of regulating births.[25] The damage to moral values is always a greater evil for the com-

23. *Gaudium et Spes,* 48.
24. *Gaudium et Spes,* 50-51. Paul I, Encyclical *Humanae Vitae,* 10 (*AAS* 60 (1968), p. 487).
25. *Gaudium et Spes,* 87. Paul VI, Encyclical *Popolorum Progressio,* 31 : Address to the United Nations, *AAS* 57 (1965), p. 883. John XXIII, *Mater et Magistra, AAS* 53 (1961), pp. 445-448). Responsible parenthood supposes the use of only morally licit methods of birth regulation. Cf. *Humanae Vitae,* 14 (*ibid.,* p. 490).

mon good than any disadvantage in the economic or demographic order.

(V) MORALITY AND LAW

(19) The moral discussion is being accompanied more or less everywhere by serious juridical debates. There is no country where legislation does not forbid and punish murder. Furthermore, many countries had specifically applied this condemnation and these penalties to the particular case of procured abortion. In these days a vast body of opinion petitions the liberalization of this latter prohibition. There already exists a fairly general tendency which seeks to limit as far as possible all restrictive legislation, especially when it seems to touch upon private life. The argument of pluralism is also used. Although many citizens – the argument goes – in particular the Catholic faithful, condemn abortion, many others hold that it is licit at least as a lesser evil. Why force them to follow an opinion which is not theirs, especially in a country where they are in the majority? In addition it is apparent that, where they still exist, the laws condemning abortion appear difficult to apply. The crime has become too common for it to be punished every time, and the pubic authorities often find that it is wiser to close their eyes to it. But the preservation of a law which is not applied is always to the detriment of authority and of all the other laws. It must be added that clandestine abortion seriously endangers the fertility and even the lives of women who resort to it. Even if the legislator continues to regard abortion as an evil, may he not propose to restrict its damage?

(20) These arguments and others in addition that are heard from varying quarters are not conclusive. It is true that civil law cannot expect to cover the whole field of morality or to punish all faults. No one expects it to do so. It must often tolerate what is in fact a lesser evil, in order to avoid a greater one. One must, however, be attentive to what a change in legislation can represent. Many will take as authorization what is perhaps only a refusal to punish. Even more, in the present case, this very refusal seems at the very least to admit that the legislator no longer considers abortion a crime against human life, since murder is still always severely punished. It is true that it is not the task of the law to choose between points of view or to impose one rather than another. But the life of the child takes precedence over all opinions. One cannot invoke freedom of thought to destroy life.

(21) The role of law is not to record what is done, but to help in promoting improvement. It is at all times the task of the State to preserve each person's rights and to protect the weakest. In order

to do so the State will have to right many wrongs. The law is not obliged to sanction everything, but it cannot act contrary to a law which is deeper and more majestic than any human law : the natural law engraved in men's hearts by the creator as a norm which reason clarifies and strives to formulate properly, and which one must always try to understand better, but which it is always wrong to contradict. Human law can abstain from punishment, but it cannot declare to be right what would be opposed to the natural law, for this opposition suffices to give the assurance that a law is not a law at all.

(22) It must in any case be clearly understood that a Christian can never conform to a law which is in itself immoral, and such is the case of a law which would admit in principle the liceity of abortion. Nor can a Christian take part in a propaganda campaign in favour of such a law, or vote for it. Moreover, he may not collaborate in its application. It is, for instance, inadmissible that doctors or nurses should find themselves obliged to co-operate closely in abortions and have to choose between the Christian law and their professional situation.

(23) On the contrary it is the task of law to pursue a reform of society and of conditions of life in all milieux, starting with the most deprived. so that always and everywhere it may be possible to give every child coming into this world a welcome worthy of a person. Help for families and for unmarried mothers, assured grants for children, legislation for illegitimate children and reasonable arrangements for adoption – a whole positive policy must be put into force so that there will always be a concrete honourable and possible alternative to abortion.

(VI) CONCLUSION

(24) Following one's conscience in obedience to the law of God is not always the easy way. One must not fail to recognize the weight of the sacrifices and the burdens which it can impose. Heroism is sometimes called for in order to remain faithful to the requirements of the divine law. Therefore we must emphasize that the path of true progress of the human person passes through this constant fidelity to a conscience maintained in uprightness and truth; and we must exhort all those who are able to do so to lighten the burdens still crushing so many men and women, families and children, who are placed in situations to which in human terms there is no solution.

(25) A Christian's outlook cannot be limited to the horizon of life in this world. He knows that during the present life another one is being prepared, one of such importance that it is in its light that

judgments must be made.[26] From this viewpoint there is no absolute misfortune here below, not even the terrible sorrow of bringing
up a handicapped child. This is the contradiction proclaimed by
the Lord : 'Happy those who mourn : they shall be comforted'
(Mt. 5:5). To measure happiness by the absence of sorrow and
misery in this world is to turn one's back on the gospel.

(26) But this does not mean that one can remain indifferent to
these sorrows and miseries. Every man and woman with feeling,
and certainly every Christian, must be ready to do what he can to
remedy them. This is the law of charity, whose first preoccupation must always be the establishment of justice. One can
never approve of abortion; but it is above all necessary to combat
its causes. This requires political action, which is the province
of the law. But it is necessary at the same time to influence
morality and to do everything possible to help families,
mothers and children. Considerable progress in the service of life
has been accomplished by medicine. One can hope that such
progress will continue : it is not a doctor's vocation to take life,
but to sustain it for as long as possible. It is also to be hoped that
help will be more and more forthcoming, either institutionalized or
by voluntary action rooted in Christian charity.

(27) One cannot effectively safeguard morality unless one
takes the fight on to the field of doctrine. A way of thinking
or, rather, an emotional prejudice against large families –
seeing them as an evil – cannot be allowed to go unchal-
lenged. It is true that all forms of civilization are not equally
favourable to large families. Industrialized and urbanized society
pose much greater difficulties for them. This is why the
Church in recent times has consistently invoked the principle of
responsible parenthood, the exercise of true human and Christian
prudence. Such prudence would not be authentic if it did not
include generosity. It must preserve awareness of the grandeur of
the task of co-operating with the Creator in the transmission of
life, which gives new members to society and new children to the
Church. A principal care and solicitude of the Church of Christ
is to protect and foster life. This applies first and foremost to the
life which Christ brought on earth : 'I have come so that they may
have life and have it to the full' (John 10 :10). But life at all its
levels comes from God, and bodily life is for man the indispensable
beginning. In this life on earth sin has introduced, multiplied and
made harder to bear suffering and death. But in taking their bur-

---

26. See Cardinal Villot, Secretary of State, to the World Congress of
Catholic Doctors held in Barrelona, 26 May 1974 (*L'Osservatore Romano,*
29 May 1974).

den upon himself Jesus Christ has transformed them : for whoever believes in him, suffering and death itself become instruments of resurrection. Hence St Paul can say : 'I think that what we suffer in this life can never be compared to the glory, as yet unrevealed, which is waiting for us' (Rom. 8:18). And, if we make this comparison we shall add with him : 'Yes, the troubles which are soon over, though they weigh little, train us for the carrying of a weight of eternal glory which is out of all proportion to them' (2 Cor. 4:17).

The Supreme Pontiff, Pope Paul VI, in an audience granted to the undersigned secretary of the Sacred Congregation for the Doctrine of the Faith on 28 June 1974 has ratified this Declaration on Procured Abortion and has confirmed it and ordered it to be promulgated.

Given in Rome, at the Sacred Congregation for the Doctrine of the Faith, on November 18, the Commemoration of the Dedication of the Basilicas of Saints Peter and Paul, in the year 1974.

FRANCISCUS CARD. SEPER (Prefect)

+HIERONYMOUS HAMER, Titular Archbishop of Lorium (Secretary)

Yes to Life[*]

ARCHBISHOPS AND BISHOPS OF IRELAND

1. Human life is sacred, even before it is born. Sexuality and sexual love are sacred, as the mysterious source of human life. These truths have been honoured by the great majority of men all through history, whatever their religion and whatever their culture.

2. Christians in particular have, until recently, been unanimous and undivided in their absolute respect for the unborn life and in their view of what reverence for sex, the source of life, implies. These values have begun to be questioned only in recent years. It is necessary for us all to examine these matters again in the light of the Gospel and in the light of Christian and human conscience.

3. It is our Christian faith which provides our deepest insight into the mystery of life and the surest guidance as to how life is to be respected. The Church has centuries of experience in dealing with men in all cultures and in all conditions. All this wise experience lies behind her judgments on human living. But her faith is much more than merely human insight: it is a sharing in the mind of Christ. St Paul says:

> We teach, not in the way in which philosophy is taught but in the way that the Spirit teaches us, showing how spiritual truths make spiritual sense . . . we are those who have the mind of Christ (1 Cor 2:13-16).

The teaching of the Church, guided by the Holy Spirit of Christ, gradually forms in us 'the same mind which was also in Christ Jesus' (Phil 2:5). We have, therefore, an obligation to form our beliefs and consciences in the full light of the teaching of the Church. This Pastoral Letter has been written in order to set out the teaching of the Church in the matter of human life and its origins in marriage.

4. The Christian principle of respect for human life at every stage of its existence is firm and clear. God alone is the Lord of life. Man is

---

[*]Extract from the pastoral letter, *Human Life Is Sacred.*

made in his image and likeness. We come from God. We go to God. We belong to God. In the Psalms we read:

Know that he, the Lord, is God.
He made us, we belong to him (Ps. 99:3).

For it was you who created my being,
knit me together in my mother's womb.
I thank you for the wonder of my being (Ps. 138:13-14).

God's commandment, 'Thou shalt not kill', unconditionally forbids all taking of innocent human life from its beginnings in the womb until the end that God, not man, has set for it. One must have absolute respect for human life as coming from God's hands at the very first moment of conception and as remaining under God's care on earth until he takes it back to himself again in death.

5. Some will argue that not every life is of equal value. But in the eyes of God every life is of equal and of priceless value. We must see every life as having the value which it has for God. Christ speaks of the loving concern for each one of us which God has as our most dear Father:

Can you not buy two sparrows for a penny? And yet not one falls to the ground without your Father knowing. Why, every hair on your head has been counted. So there is no need to be afraid; you are worth more than hundreds of sparrows (Matt 10:29-31).

Each human being is called to live with God forever. Each human being is one of whom Christ thought so much that he died for him. Here is where each human being gets his value. Some people have answered the question, 'What is that man worth?', by stating the value of his assets or the amount of his annual earnings. The true answer is: 'That man is worth the life's blood of Christ'. There and only there is the true standard for judging the value of life.

6. Secular society has different priorities in its attitudes and laws. In many countries State law has come to allow abortion for a variety of reasons. The changes in the law which brought this about would not have been introduced unless public opinion had first been lulled by propaganda; but when changes of this kind in the law are introduced they change public opinion still further and much more rapidly in the same direction. Abortion is now discussed in many

countries almost as if it raised no moral problem at all. People talk now instead as if the only problem were to find ways of making abortion still more widely available, faster and cheaper.

7. In this Letter, we are speaking primarily on the basis of our faith in Christ. We are speaking primarily to those who share that faith. But we confidently appeal also to the 'unwritten laws' of the Creator, which can be seen by human reason to be written in God's creation, and to be engraved in the heart of man, in his conscience and his sense of personal responsibility. During the whole of its history until very recently, and even before Christianity, the ethics of the medical profession found its cherished expression in the Hippocratic Oath. By the terms of this Oath, already five hundred years before Christ, doctors solemnly swore:

> I shall never, no matter who may demand it, supply a homicidal drug ... I shall never supply any woman with an abortive pessary. By chastity and sanctity, I shall protect my life and my profession.

A more modern form of this Oath, the Geneva Medical Oath, drawn up in 1948 by the World Health Organisation, says:

> I shall keep absolute respect for human life, from the moment of conception.

We are therefore at one with the oldest and noblest traditions of the medical profession when we take our stand for the sacred character and the absolute rights of unborn life. We are also at one with the deepest convictions of the human conscience.

8. When the Church states her moral principles, however, she appeals ultimately to the truth and love which Christ brought into the world. She takes the Divine Teacher as her model. She endeavours to speak clearly and without compromise; but she speaks with love for the human person, with respect for human intellect and for human freedom; and she speaks with the confidence that the inner force of the Christian message will, by God's grace, and because of its sheer truth and rightness, find an answering echo in the heart of man.

ABORTION IS KILLING THE INNOCENT

9. God's commandment, as we have seen, is that no human being may deliberately take away innocent human life. What life could be

more innocent than that of the unborn child? Deliberate abortion is therefore always gravely sinful. The embryo or foetus possesses its fundamental right to life from the moment of conception. From that moment the foetus is already provided with all the genetic elements which will shape its future development as an adult human person. To use the language of genetics, the embryo, from the instant of the meeting of the mother and father cells, is already equipped with the entire 'programme' of its future physical characteristics, right down to the minutest detail (including its unique and identifying finger-prints), as well as of its basic mental capacity and personality traits. Everything that education and environment will later have to work on is already present in the embryo. Each single embryo, even though so small as to be invisible to the naked eye, is unique and un-repeatable. Strictly speaking, so far as in-built potential for future development is concerned, the newly-fertilised mother-cell has the same potential as the newly-born baby. A distinguished Professor of Midwifery has said:

> This is more than a potential human being; it is already a human being with potential, complete with every genetic detail, unique, individual and unrepeatable.

From the day of conception to the day of birth, life in the womb is a continuing process of inter-locking events. To interrupt the process is to take innocent human life.

10. How could women and girls ever think of having an abortion performed if they realised the wonder and the beauty of the tiny being that is living and growing close to their heart? How can men be so heartlessly insensitive to the deepest feelings of women, so blind to the mysteries of parenthood, as to pressurise their partners into seeking abortions? Once their child is conceived, they are not about to become parents: they have become parents already. Any mother who has had the sorrow of a miscarriage knows that it was a baby that she lost.

11. The likeness of the parents is already stamped on the little being from the beginning. The human organs and features develop with astonishing rapidity. Before the first month is out, head and brain-cells, mouth and eyes are there. By the end of the fourth week, the beating of the heart has been detected. In the sixth or seventh week, the foetus will respond to a touch. Many abortions take place at twelve weeks. By then the baby has well developed features and its heart-beat can be easily identified. Two hearts are then beating

together in the mother's body; but the small heart depends entirely on the large one, not only for the blood supply which brings it nourishment, but even more for the love which will allow it to develop its full human potential.

12. Any form of abortion, however early it is performed and by whatever expert, is so crude and brutal as hardly to bear description. One method is for the little body to be 'scraped out', that is to say cut up within the womb and pulled out in pieces with a forceps. Alternatively and more often the body is 'sucked out' in parts by vacuum extraction. A third method — though this one tends to be avoided now as carrying risk to the mother — was to replace the fluid in which the baby lives by a salt or glucose solution; this burned up the foetus or killed it slowly by poisoning, and it was born dead some time afterwards by a false labour. At later stages of the pregnancy, the baby is removed from the mother by a surgical operation. When lifted out of its home in the mother's womb, it is still alive. After a while it dies of exposure. People speak of a non-viable baby (one which cannot live outside the womb) as being not yet human. Let us not forget that any one of us would be non-viable if unable to walk and left out for long enough without clothing in the snow.

13. It is not pleasant to speak of these matters. The facts of abortion are ugly. But they are the facts. It is dishonest to conceal them, or to speak of them in impersonal clinical phrases like 'termination of pregnancy', 'scraping the uterine lining', 'emptying the uterus', and so on. Smooth words will not change evil things into good. Killing a baby is still killing a baby even if people call it 'termination of pregnancy', or more smoothly, 'deconception'. For a man to kill his next-door neighbour is still murder, even if the man says he is only 'terminating the occupancy of the adjoining residence'.

14. Abortion does not become in any degree less ugly or less evil if some State law permits it or if it is done in a public hospital by a specialist under a government health service. Mothers who consent to have this done have usually not been allowed to know, or have not permitted themselves to think, about what it is that is being done to their baby. At seminars and discussions promoting abortion, lecturers impress upon nursing personnel that mothers are never in any circumstances to be told what the operation involves, and that the word 'baby' is strictly never to be used in their hearing. It is to be replaced by such impersonal terms as 'fetal parts', 'fetal tissue', 'contents of the uterus', etc. In this same connection, it is significant that research in America has found a high incidence of anxiety and

guilt-feeling among para-medical personnel involved in abortions. This is true particularly among nurses. The occurrence of anxiety and guilt-feelings is related to the closeness of involvement in the actual abortion operation. One report states:

> The effect of actual observation and participation in the abortion procedure appears to be a powerful determinant in activating anxiety-producing psychological processes.

This report goes on to recommend that social workers involved in abortion work be so trained that they can help the other personnel involved to overcome their 'negative emotional reactions'. The technique recommended for doing this is to direct their attention away from the foetus, the operation and its result, and to divert it to the problems of the mother.

15. It should be noted that the lobby which campaigned for legalised abortion in Britain planned their propaganda very carefully and selected their themes very skilfully. They made a deliberate decision to concentrate on the 'hard cases'. The campaign was led by a body called the Abortion Law Reform Association. Two of the members of this body wrote a book about their campaign. One of the things they say is this:

> There was (and still is) so much latent public distaste for the very idea of abortion that it was obvious throughout the Reform Campaign that they would only be able to carry the country with them if they concentrated on the hard cases.

The same two writers make a number of other revealing statements. They point out that the Association made great play with opinion surveys. They admit that in the area of abortion 'almost all figures were (and still are) subject to dispute'; but they go on to say that the organisers of the campaign discovered that opinion surveys were, as they very candidly put it, a 'match-winning tactic'. Another successful tactic, they report, was to involve the women's organisations in the movement. Every move depended, of course, on the help of the media, and this was willingly forthcoming. Our two authors recorded with delight that 'the mass-circulation newspapers realised that abortion was a popular subject', and that from the moment this realisation dawned, 'every event was eagerly gobbled up and disgorged by press, radio and television'. Finally, and this was the most important point of all, the Association worked hard and successfully at, as they put it, 'lining up friends at the centre of power'. It is useful to bear in mind these hints from inside the movement about how a successful lobby in the area of public morality is worked.

RIGHTS OF THE UNBORN

16. People who support abortion speak as if the unborn baby had no rights. Yet, if a father dies before his child is born, regardless of what the stage of the pregnancy, the child when born has legal rights of inheritance. In the case of the thalidomide babies, babies injured between the time of conception and birth were found entitled to compensation. Recently the English Law Commission recommended that compensation be claimable for unborn babies injured in the womb by the fault of another. The United Nations Organisation in 1959 declared:

> The child, because of its physical and mental immaturity, needs special care and safeguards, including legal safeguards, before as well as after birth.

Considerable embarrassment is caused to legal people by the effort to reconcile these facts with the law permitting the killing of unborn babies.

17. Recently some philosophers and theologians have argued that the person becomes a person only when recognised as such by the community. They call this an act of 'humanisation'. To refuse birth to a child, they claim, simply means that it is not being accepted or recognised as a person, and that therefore it is not a person. But the point is that we are not free to refuse to recognise another human being as a person. Refusal to recognise another human being as a person is in fact the essence of all immorality in human relations. It is the basis of all oppression, torture, denial of civil rights, religious and racial discrimination, exploitation, all forms of inhumanity of man to man. All of these are simply ways of refusing to recognise other human beings as human. Once human life exists, we are *morally bound* to respect its right to life, to development, to human dignity. Otherwise, the very basis of morality is undermined.

18. The earliest Christian writers had no hesitation in calling abortion murder, no matter at what stage of the pregnancy it was performed. One writer, Tertullian, already in the second century, said:

To prevent birth is anticipated murder; it makes little difference whether one destroys a life already born or does away with it in its nascent stage. The one who is to become a man is already a man.

19. In any case, modern genetic science makes it more difficult to deny that the human soul is present from the moment of conception. As we have pointed out earlier, the embryo, from the first instant, possesses all the genetic characteristics of the adult. The programme for future development is already laid down on the first day of unborn life. The adventure of every human life begins in the womb. The foetus could never become human if it were not human already. The view which is most in harmony with modern science is that the spiritual soul is present from the first moment of conception.

CONSEQUENCES OF ABORTION

20. When discussing abortion in the past, people used to speak of the cruel dilemma of 'choice' between the life of the mother, which could be endangered by the continuance of the pregnancy, and the life of her unborn child. Such cases were always extremely few in number. We thank God that nowadays, where modern obstetric facilities are available, such cases are almost non-existent. It is strange that the pressure for abortion should have come principally from those countries where medical science is most advanced; for in fact advances in medicine and progress in ante-natal and obstetric services had eliminated most of the cases in which pregnancy could be a danger to the life of the mother.

21. The statistics from countries which have legalised abortion are revealing in this regard. The 'indications' for which abortion is sought and obtained are for the most part of a psychological, social or economic kind, rather than based on grounds of physical danger or disease. Figures for England show that the 'life or death' situation applied to only a tiny fraction of the total number of abortions. Taken together, all cases that could for any reason, whether medical of psychological, be really called 'hard cases', account for not more than 2 per cent of all the registered abortions carried out in England in recent years.

22. Some abortions are now performed on the grounds of the likelihood of the child's being born defective or handicapped. This, however, even if it could be demonstrated with certainty, would still not justify the deliberate killing of the innocent. It may be hard to see

the meaning of a handicapped child's life, and hard for parents to accept it, if they do not look at life on earth with the eyes of faith. But if we judge life and its worth by the standards of physical health and worldly welfare alone, then we have quite simply turned our backs upon the Gospel of Christ. In any case, those who have not experienced it will never know the amount of consolation that has been brought to parents in reward for the stress of caring for their handicapped child. The capacity for affection of many of these children is the joy of their parents' hearts. History will never calculate the amount of good that has been brought into our world by the devotion of parents and the care of the wider community in coping with the problems of handicapped children. Great progress has been made recently in social attitudes to this problem and in social provision for it. Great advances have ben made in the education of children suffering from all forms of handicap. This is one outstanding example of how society can uplift itself by accepting and coping with suffering. Abortion, on the other hand, is a striking instance of how society can degrade and perhaps destroy itself by systematic refusal of suffering.

23. Abortion does not even succeed in eliminating suffering. It has to be remembered that God has provided in the mother's body quite remarkable systems of security and protection for the unborn child during all the stages of the pregnancy. Interference with these systems can be injurious to the mother as well as fatal to the child. These systems include instincts deeply embedded in the mother's personality. Abortion, by violating these womanly instincts, can lead in the long run to psychological disturbance to the mother. Some researchers have reported a notable proportion of mothers who suffer emotional disturbance after the abortion. Many suffer, in one degree or another, from guilt-feelings. There is a tendency, in much of the discussion about abortions, to ignore such findings. They are likely to be verified particularly, of course, in countries of Christian and especially Catholic background; but similar reports have come from non-Christian countries like Japan. It should be noted too that a high proportion of legal abortions are sanctioned for psychiatric reasons; but it is known that those mothers who are severely emotionally disturbed by a pregnancy are precisely the ones who are more likely to be disturbed by post-abortion doubts and guilt-feelings. Research also suggests that some harmful physical effects for the mother herself and some risks for her future pregnancies can be traced to abortion.

LEGALISATION INCREASES DEMAND

24. Since the Abortion Act came into force in Britain in 1967, the number of abortions notified has risen steadily year by year, going from 25,000 in 1968 to 170,000 in 1973. The figures speak for themselves. As the law stands at present, the situation seems to come very close to abortion on demand. And all this, it should be noted, is happening in a country where there is widespread availability and use of contraceptives. The two pro-abortion writers whom we quoted earlier point out that:

> the problem (of unwanted children) is actually getting worse, despite the universal availability of contraceptives.

They argue:

> Abortion on request is a logical concomitant of contraception on demand.

Availability of contraception will not lessen recourse to abortion: it will only spread still further the mentality and style of life which produce the demand for abortion. There are no easy options to take the place of moral living.

25. Some people sincerely believe that a legal measure of control would at least reduce the number of criminal abortions, with all the appalling risks and problems which these are causing. There are indications, however, that criminal abortions are continuing, side by side with the legal abortions. This has also been the experience in other countries with a longer history than Britain of legalised abortion. Furthermore, abusive practices operating under the actual cover of the law have often gone far to remove the distinction between criminal and legal abortions.

26. A responsible society would surely find other ways of coping with the problem of criminal abortions than simply to try to introduce legal abortion. Protection for unborn life should be part of society's whole commitment to the improvement of the quality of human life. There is a strange contrast in modern society between the genuine compassion which lies behind movements to abolish capital punishment and to reform the whole penal code for offenders, on the one hand, and, on the other, the barbarous killing of unborn babies. Indeed, the more one thinks of the terrible crime which abortion is, the more one finds that it is in complete contradiction with everything

that a caring and compassionate society wishes to be. Modern society sincerely wishes and tries to be caring and compassionate. How can one explain the contradiction? One seems forced to the conclusion that sexual freedom has become such an obsession with modern society that it will sacrifice anything, even unborn babies, to appease this new absolute.

"YES" TO LIFE

27. The Constitution *On the Church in the Modern World* of Vatican II declared:

> God has conferred on man the surpassing ministry of safeguarding life, a ministry which must be fulfilled in a manner worthy of man. Therefore, from the moment of conception, life must be guarded with the greatest care — abortion and infanticide are unspeakable crimes.

28. But we should not just say that the Church is 'against abortion'. We should say that the Church is *for* life. The Church says 'Yes' to life. The Church has been saying 'Yes' to unborn life, without any hesitation or reservation, for two thousand years. In recent years, since the abortion debate became a public issue in country after country, nearly every Catholic Hierarchy in Europe, in America and everywhere the issue has been raised, has responded by once more clearly and strongly and unanimously repeating this great 'Yes' to unborn life.

29. In Ireland, we are far from being unaffected by the problem and by the accompanying discussion. Experience elsewhere, as we have already indicated, shows only too clearly what carefully organised pressure-groups can do to confuse and then to change public opinion. More immediately disturbing is the fact that considerable numbers of Irish girls are already going to England each year to have abortions performed. At present more than 2,200 Irish girls are officially registered as having abortions in Britain each year. More than half of these are from the Republic. Since the introduction of legal abortion, probably at least 8,000 Irish-resident girls and women have had abortions under the British Act. Over half of these are from the Republic. This clearly could not be happening without encouragement and advice from people they consult in this country. Those who advise or arrange abortions for girls and women who consult them bear as great, if not a greater degree of guilt than the

girls and women themselves. These figures indicate widespread moral confusion and lack of knowledge. This is the context in which we write this Letter.

30. As we write it, we are aware of the agonies of conscience and the tortures of remorse which many girls who have had abortions are now suffering. We want to speak to them too. We want to assure them of the boundless compassion and unlimited mercy of Christ. He loves them. He loves to forgive. He has told us that he has more joy in forgiving sinners than he receives from the just who do not think they need forgiveness. No-one is excluded from his love. No matter what the past, he offers everyone forgiveness and peace. His 'Yes' to life is also an unconditional 'Yes' to all who come in sorrow and love to ask his pardon.

THE QUALITY OF LIFE

31. The Church says 'Yes', not just to human existence, but to the quality and dignity of human life. The Christian demand is that all human life should be permitted and enabled to develop to the full dignity and quality of living which befit a human person and child of God. Nothing less than that is what is commanded by Christ's command to love our neighbour as we love our own self. The Christian 'Yes' to life includes a call for freedom, for adequate education, for proper living conditions, for more just distribution of wealth and opportunity, for protection of the human environment, and for more responsible use of the resources of nature. The Church is not simply 'against abortion'; she is *for* life and *for* man and *for* human dignity and social justice.

32. It is often said nowadays that we should not consider so much the mere existence of life, but rather the quality which that life has the prospect of attaining. Some argue that unless unborn life can be assured of a certain quality, then the mere fact of its existence is deprived of value. Or that if the existence of unborn life seriously lessens the prospect of an acceptable quality of life for the mother or her family, then the unborn life cannot be said to have a right to exist.

33. This argument turns moral principles upside down. Life has the right to quality and dignity because it exists. Life does not derive the right to exist from the quality which circumstances seem likely to give to it. Once human life exists, then those who conceived it have the obligation to respect its right to continue to exist. They have, at the same time, the obligation to create the conditions which will enable it to develop in a manner worthy of its human dignity. If

parents cannot themselves ensure this, then society has the strict duty to come to their help with all the supports that are necessary to give this new life a quality corresponding to its sacred character as a human person, made in the image of God.

Abortion and the Right to Life

ARCHBISHOPS OF GREAT BRITAIN

(1) We, the Catholic archbishops of Great Britain, address this joint statement on abortion to our fellow Christians and indeed to our fellow-citizens of every religion and none.

(2) We speak in defence of life against the evil of abortion. We speak in a society where all enjoy a freedom which is rightly prized and which was affirmed by the Catholic Church in the second Vatican Council; a full freedom of religious belief and practice, and a freedom to seek the truth about everything including moral matters. We live in a society where many differing moral and political opinions are conscientiously held and pursued in practice. We make no attempt to override the consciences of our fellow-citizens. We do not seek to have all Catholic moral teaching imposed by law, or even adopted as public policy.

(3) But we too have the right, as members of this pluralistic society, to appeal to the consciences not only of our fellow-Catholics, but also of our fellow-citizens and our political leaders and representatives. We too have consciences. And we cannot in conscience remain silent while the most basic human beings are ignored and overridden by the law and, increasingly, by the public policies and everyday practices of our country. These developing human lives may be unborn and silent but they are already our neighbours, living in our midst and are part of our human family. They need to be defended.

AN ISSUE OF BASIC HUMAN RIGHTS AND DIGNITY

(4) The Church speaks out against abortion, as it has from the beginning, because it acknowledges the human rights and dignity of all, including the unborn, and is committed to their defence. There is here a crucial point of principle. It has everything to do with the intrinsic value and inalienable rights of each individual. It is a matter of respect for our neighbour.

(5) Our stand against abortion is one aspect of our stand against all practices that degrade human rights and dignity. Scottish bishops have made many statements, both individually and collectively, on the need to aid developing nations, on social justice at home and

abroad, on unemployment problems and on help for the needy and deprived. The bishops of England and Wales issued in 1971 a major statement on moral questions which ranged over Christian living, race relations, violence and peace. Since then the bishops have tackled the housing problem, disarmament and many current social issues. The bishops have tried to defend the insulted, the despised, the disadvantaged. With other Christians we have resisted racism. We have stressed the brotherhood of man and rejected any discrimination based on colour or race.

(6) The whole of Christian social teaching can be seen as an appeal to the conscience of the relatively well-off and powerful to give practical recognition to the humanity and rights of the poor and the weak. And that social teaching proclaims as well the rights of minorities against majorities who treat them with unfair indifference or hostility.

(7) More often than not the expected child is wanted and welcomed by parents and family and is later received without question by the community at large. But when we look at the law of our land, when we reflect on the practices which result in over 140,000 registered abortions a year, when we note the changing attitudes of many who work in health care, we feel obliged to say: unborn children in Great Britain are today a legally disadvantaged class; they are weak; they are a minority. So they are entitled to be defended by anyone of humane conscience, but also, particularly, by those who, like us, profess that every human being without exception has the unique dignity of an eternal destiny.

PROTECTING THE INNOCENT AGAINST DIRECT ATTACKS

(8) What we have to say about abortion is consistent with the whole Christian teaching about the right of the innocent to live. That teaching is central to our civilisation. Without it, no other human rights are secure. Sometimes there are occasions when individuals or nations, in self-defence, may rightly use force, even deadly force, against anyone who by his own use of a similar degree of force is unjustly attacking them. But the right of self-defence is limited; it never entitles us directly to kill the innocent, that is those who are not contributing to the unjust attack.

(9) This is why the second Vatican Council emphatically declared that every warlike act directed to the indiscriminate destruction of whole cities or large areas with their inhabitants is a crime. The reason for that teaching is that any such act, because indiscriminate,

would inevitably involve a direct attack on the life of innocent inhabitants of these cities or other areas.

(10) The Catholic teaching on abortion is no more than one application of the fundamental teaching that the innocent may not be directly attacked.

EACH OF THE UNBORN IS A UNIQUE, HUMAN INDIVIDUAL

(11) Even before the processes of human reproduction became well understood, Christian teaching always regarded the unborn, at all stages of pregnancy, as possessed of a distinct, new life which no one could rightly seek to destroy. For many centuries, Christians like others took for granted scientific and philosophical theories which suggested that the newly-conceived human being did not become formed or ensouled until several weeks after conception. So in those times the ecclesiastical penalties and censures for causing an abortion early in a pregnancy were often less severe than those for abortion in later pregnancy. But throughout those centuries, the Church never wavered in its teaching that abortion, at whatever stage of pregnancy, is seriously wrongful. Today the course of human development is much better understood. Modern science enables us to see better than ever before the fundamental significance of the time of conception.

(12) For at the time of conception there comes into existence a new life. There is a union in which a living cell from the father fertilises a living cell from the mother. That union, a transmission of life, is the beginning of new life. Usually this new life is and will always remain a single individual; sometimes, in ways not fully understood, there may then or a few days later be division resulting, for example, in identical twins. But scientists can tell us that, from the time of conception, the features which distinguish us from each of our parents – the colour of our eyes, our shape of face, and so on – are all laid down in the 'genetic code' that comes into existence then. Each such new life is the life not of a potential human being but of a human being with potential. The development of this potential is normally a process of profound continuity. No one can point to, say, the fourth week of that process, or the eighth, the twelfth, the twentieth, the twenty-fourth or twenty-eighth, and say: 'That is when I began being me'. Birth itself is certainly an event in the life-story of each one of us. But for the beginning of that story we must look to the time of our conception.

(13) The unborn child has not yet developed all its potentialities, and it is dependent on its mother. But the newlyborn infant too is dependent and even adults have not yet developed all their potentialities. Scientists can tell us more and more details of the ways in

which the bodily organisation of the growing child in the womb is, from the beginning, biologically distinct and clearly separate from the pregnant woman's body, which is physically contributing to, sustaining and embracing her child's. It makes nonsense to speak of this living and developing being as simply a part of the woman's body. Medical technology can reveal to us the early stages of the child's heartbeat, brainwaves, muscular movement, sensitivity to touch — all within a few weeks of conception. We believe that all this is becoming more and more widely known. Certainly it deserves to be known, for the development and essential completion of the bodily constitution of the child in the womb is one of the wonders of this created universe. And this knowledge helps to break down the prejudice that the human community consists of those already born or viable. That prejudice is the root of the newly respectable yet still unjust discrimination which is abortion.

ABORTION IS UNFAIR DISCRIMINATION

(14) Much is made in society today of woman's rights and within the abortion debate much is made of a woman's rights over her own body. No doubt we all have certain moral rights but, of course, no rights are unlimited. The question of a woman's rights in respect of her own body is too often put as a one-sided slogan which is deceptive and which ignored consideration for others and for the bodily rights of others. Many responsibilities arise from the need to respect the rights of others.

(15) Since men and women have rights in respect of their own bodies, children have such rights too. It does not matter whether we call our children 'neonates' (the medical term for those just born), or 'fetuses' (the medical term for the unborn in mid or late-pregnancy), or 'embryos' (a medical term for the unborn in all earlier stages of pregnancy); the fact remains that the young and growing offspring of human parents are children. Unborn children have rights in respect of their own bodies, even while they are enclosed within and sustained by their mothers' bodies.

(16) What is their right? It is the right not to be made the object of attack. So the course of their development before birth must not be interfered with by any procedure or technical process carried out with the intention of preventing the continuation of that development. When we speak of abortion and condemn any attempt to procure it, we are referring to any procedure or technique which is adopted with that intention. Interference with the unborn child just in order to get

rid of it would obviously be abortion, even if one did not positively want to kill it but acted regardless of the certainty or risk that it would thereby die. If a technique or device achieves such effects after conception, it is in fact an abortifacient, an abortion-device, even if it is often called by other names, such as 'contraceptive' or 'menstrual extraction' and so on.

(17) Some abortions, perhaps many, appear to be performed for reasons which are basically selfish or even trivial. Others are the results of strong social and psychological pressure. Lack of support, or even hostility, from the father of the child, especially if the pregnancy is seen as a failure in the use of contraception, may leave the mother abandoned and despairing. A similar attitude of re-crimination from parents or friends can drive a lonely unmarried girl to a final decision which in her heart she does not really want. In many such cases it is difficult to think of abortion as in any full sense a free choice on the part of the mother against her defenceless unborn child and also against her deeper instincts of preservation and love for her offspring. Honest recognition by others of their duties and responsibilities towards the pregnant woman and her child would often remove the pressures driving towards abortion.

JUSTICE FOR THE UNBORN

(18) Termination of pregnancy by induced abortion means death for the unborn. It means killing. That is what is offered as the solution to problems of inconvenience or embarrassment, or of some risk to the mental or physical well-being of the mother or perhaps of her other children. To condemn such a solution as we do is not to minimise those problems. But we cannot shirk the fact that bringing up children after their birth can likewise cause problems of inconvenience, embarrassment, poverty and risk to their parents and brothers and sisters. The 'moral' arguments for abortion can equally be used as arguments for infanticide, for killing children after birth. That is the logic which the pagan world before Christ followed to its conclusion; the 'exposure' that is killing by act or neglect of unwanted or inconvenient children after birth. It has to be recognised that neither birth, nor viability, makes any real difference to the intrinsic rights of a human being. Our civilisation still makes a moral judgment about our responsibilities to young children after birth. We all say that they are entitled to care and rescue even at the cost of hard and thankless work or even risk. The same judgment has to be made

about our responsibilities to those other children still unborn but who differ only in the degree of their development.

(19) These considerations of justice are real and valid. We realise that to many people they will seem hard and unfeeling. The pregnant girl or woman experiences her situation with all its difficulties and may see her unborn child as a threat rather than as a living human being. Those among whom she lives are aware of her present problems which may cry out for practical measures of relief and support. The unborn child, on the other hand, remains unseen and unheard, with a life and destiny which only the future can bring to light. It takes a vigorous effort of imagination and of clear, 'hard' thinking to appreciate that the unborn child has a claim which cannot be outweighed by inconveniences and risks and a life which cannot fairly be sacrificed for reasons of health; the unborn child has a claim which calls for the respect due to a living human being.

THE HANDICAPPED ARE ENTITLED TO LIVE

(20) But what about a child who will or may be born handicapped in mind or body? Here again we must be clear. No one has a right to kill another human on the basis that that other would be 'better off dead'. Once we see that the child before birth is not essentially different from the child after birth, we are also forced to conclude that selective abortion, that is killing unborn children to save them from a life of handicap, is also to be condemned. Such selective abortions are equivalent to asserting the essential rightness of euthanasia — the killing of the aged, infirm or handicapped, with or without their consent, because someone judges that they would be better off dead. And these abortions are profoundly at odds with the caring work for handicapped children and adults to which so many of our fellow-Christians and fellow-citizens have devoted and are devoting so much of their lives. Many handicapped people are themselves deeply opposed to abortion, having discovered for themselves the inner richness of human existence.

PARTICULARLY HARD CASES

(21) *Rape.* We speak with equal feeling about the bodily rights of women and of their unborn, perhaps unwanted offspring. People sometimes argue that abortions are justified if a child is conceived as a consequence of rape. Who can adequately express the outrage suffered by the victim of a rape? A woman is certainly entitled to defend

herself against the continuing effects of such an attack and to seek immediate medical assistance with a view to preventing conception. In a very small number of cases, conception may in fact occur. Then there exists a new being whose individuality, distinct from each of its parents and from any of their cells, we have already described. From that time, the requirements of the moral law, transcending even the most understandable emotional reactions, are clear; the newly-conceived child cannot rightly be made to suffer the penalty of death for a man's violation of the woman.

(22) *Danger of death of the mother.* Catholic teaching on abortion accords fully with principles of moral reasonableness. The abortion that must be judged always unacceptable to the upright moral conscience is the direct abortion that we described earlier (para 16); those procedures and techniques that are intended to stop the unborn child's continuing development. We are not speaking of cases where the interference with the unborn child is in fact an unintended, though foreseen, side-effect of procedures necessary to save the mother from some underlying or supervening condition that threatens her life. For example, a treatment for cancer of the uterus can be justified even if it also causes a miscarriage. Even in such cases, however, it is the doctor's duty to regard both the mother and the unborn child as his patients, and to try to sustain the pregnancy so long as there is any reasonable prospect of saving both of them.

(23) If there remain any cases, which in contemporary medicine are certainly exceedingly rare or perhaps even non-existent, in which the life of the mother could not be saved without a direct abortion, a sensitive and upright conscience must in these cases be guided by the fundamental principles which govern all these matters; innocent life is not to be directly attacked; the unborn child has an intrinsic right to life.

(24) In such a situation, the law of God, which is also the rule of reason, makes exceptionally high demands. In reaffirming that law we are not asserting that the law of the land should treat as criminal the acts of someone who, in that situation, does not acknowledge or does not live up to those demands. But we point out, once again, that what we have to say about abortion is but one application of wider principles. The principles that the Church proclaims are not for some ideal or theoretical world or for humanity in the abstract. They speak directly to the consciences of men and women in this world. They are principles that can on occasion demand heroic self-sacrifice of individuals and nations. For there are situations, for example in war, in which self-defence could not be effective without the commission of

acts which must never be done, whatever the consequences. Innocent hostages, for example, must never be killed. And having said all that, we may add that the truly practical and pressing problem in modern Britain is not the tiny proportion of cases in which the mother's life is in jeopardy. The real problem is rather this. The vast majority of abortions carried out in Great Britain represent a massive and growing trivialisation of human life, an increasing acceptance of the practice of killing on demand.

LAW AND PRACTICE IN BRITAIN

(25) *The law of the land.* We have said (para 2) that the Catholic Church does not ask that the law of the land should coincide in every respect with the moral law. And, in relation to abortion, we have just mentioned (para 24) a situation in which the requirements of the criminal law might reasonably be less demanding than those of a truly moral conscience. As Catholic archbishops of Great Britain we do not intend now to make a complete commentary on either the present or the ideal state of the law on abortion. But we will say three things:

(1) Law ought to uphold and embody the principles that are basic to our civilisation and our existing law in every other field; innocent life is to be protected by the criminal law and public policy; no law should countenance discrimination by the strong against the weak.

(2) The present law, the Abortion Act 1967, is grossly unjust. It permits the killing of the unborn because of some 'substantial risk' that they may suffer some 'serious handicap'. It wrongly presumes that such people can be treated as if they were 'better off dead'.

(3) The Abortion Act's criterion for lawful abortion is essentially the same criterion as any doctor would use in any operation when only one patient is at stake: 'Will operating involve greater risks than not operating?' Thus, apart from some extra paperwork, our law seems to put abortion on a par with cosmetic operations. It treats the presence of a new human being as insignificant. It treats the very life and existence of that new human being as out-weighed in value by another human being's perhaps slight or passing problems of physical or mental well-being.

In both these ways, the Abortion Act 1967 departs fundamentally from the most basic tradition of our law: the innocent and weak, as much as the powerful and healthy, are entitled to the equal protection of the law.

(26) *Conscience and medical practice.* Having spoken about the existing law as it affects the unborn and those who have to deal with them, we must say something about the way this law is tending in practice to affect medical personnel because of their conscientiously-held beliefs about the rights of the innocent to live. It is hard to deny that there are talented and devoted men and women who are, in effect, being debarred, or at least seriously deterred, from pursuing their chosen speciality, not only in obstetrics and gynaecology but in other medical spheres closely related to the abortion procedure. Simple reform of the conscientious-objection clauses of the Abortion Act 1967 would not be enough to put an end to this deplorable development. Positive administrative action should be instituted both in hospitals and the community services to ensure that the many thousands already engaged are not indirectly induced to act in conflict with their deepest convictions. Employing authorities should not require participation in the abortion procedure as a necessary condition of employment.

POSITIVE RESPONSIBILITIES OF CHRISTIANS AND OF SOCIETY

(27) A stand against abortion is a stand for humanity. It therefore involves a stand for women, particularly those who are or who may be pregnant. Whether or not her pregnancy results from her inadequate awareness of the moral significance of sexual intercourse, a girl or woman should always be given the practical help she may need to carry through her pregnancy. She should be given it unstintingly and without moral censure. The help may include counselling and advice, for example about the possible adoption of her baby, or about bringing up a one-parent family. But it must always be given in a way that fully respects her freedom and responsibility.

(28) Very necessary and very encouraging are the efforts of those voluntary associations in which Catholics and non-Catholics work together to attack abortion at its root by providing moral and material support to any and every mother-to-be who is willing to allow her baby to be born and not aborted. Many of our own dioceses have pledged themselves to provide such help, confidentially and at no expense to the woman; this help includes, if she wishes, the care for her baby after birth. But more, much more, will need to be

done, by Catholics and by all who care about mother and child alike. Governments and local authorities, too, are not entitled to look to abortion to relieve them from their responsibilities, for example to tackle the problems caused by shortage of housing. Still less may they treat abortion as a 'solution' to problems of overcrowded schooling, one-parent families, and juvenile delinquency. Calculations of cost-effectiveness and drives for economy must always be subordinate to basic principles of human rights.

A WORD OF ENCOURAGEMENT

(29) To all who are working *against* abortion and *for* the life and future of the unborn and their distressed mothers, we say: do not be discouraged. The laws, practices and opinions of our society may seem, at times, all too firmly set in favour of abortion. Substantial reform may at times seem beyond reach — let alone the full justice which you seek. But your work is not in vain. At the very least it preserves our society from greater and more rapid corruption. At the very least it also preserves for everyone an option that would otherwise become stifled and forgotten; the option — of pregnant women and their relatives and friends, of doctors, of nurses, of social workers — to respect innocent life and to refuse to take part in its destruction. And at best, your efforts may well be crowned with success. Success has so often appeared to social reformers to be beyond their reach, almost up to the moment when they attained it.

A CALL TO COMMITMENT

(30) By practising and condoning abortion, our society has lost its way. Each one of us must ask what we have done and are doing to help show the way to those of our fellow-citizens who have lost their bearings in this matter. If we are in medical practice, nursing or social work, have we really stood firm? If we are teachers, have we taught without compromise? If we are young and eager for justice, have we extended our concern to our neighbours, the unborn? Very many of us must now recognise that we have not done enough. Now is the time for those of goodwill to commit themselves, in one way or another, to work *against* abortion and *for* the life and future of the unborn and their distressed mothers.

(31) To our fellow-Catholics we can add this: when we acknowledge and respect the sanctity of human life we are acknowledging both the unique value of every human individual

made in the image and likeness of God, and the domination of God over that life and over its creation and its ending. Work against abortion and for the life of the unborn and their distressed mothers is a work of true charity, of everlasting significance. As Pope John Paul II, in his first encyclical, *Redemptor hominis,* recalls (para 16), we must all be mindful of the scene of the last judgment according to the words of Christ related to Matthew's Gospel (Matt 25:31-46). Going beyond those words to their wider meaning, we must suppose that when that day of judgment comes, the Lord will confront those who without justice, mercy or repentance killed the innocent unborn. But he will also address those who tried to save the lives of those innocents. And to them, we may surely suppose, the Lord will say: 'Inasmuch as you defended the least of these, you defended me'.

Medical Ethics
in the Pluralist State[1]

BRENDAN O'MAHONY, O.F.M.Cap.

PRELIMINARIES
1. I wish to make it very clear from the start that I am not speaking as Provincial of the Capuchins; and that the views I express are *personal*. I speak rather from a philosophical and theological background.
2. The 'Pluralist State' I have in mind is the Republic of Ireland — 'a sovereign, independent, democratic state'.[2]
3. I have no intention of tackling the intricate problem of the many meanings attributed to the term 'pluralist society' or to explore the limits of freedom in a pluralist society.[3]

I. THE PLURALIST STATE

The basic values in a pluralist society are firstly, *freedom* (of religion, of conscience, of expression), not an unrestricted or absolute freedom for all possible views, because some would be mutually exclusive and infringe on other freedoms; and, secondly, *tolerance,* which requires the people to recognise, accept and respect those values and world-views which differ from their own. This should not be a negative or grudging tolerance in the sense of 'putting up with' others, but rather a conviction that society is enriched by this

---

1. This paper was delivered at the invitation of the Medical Commission of the 'Conference of Major Religious Superiors of Ireland' (CMRSI) at St John of God Conference Centre, Stillorgan, Dublin, on 13th May 1982. It was delivered to Major Superiors involved in the Medical Apostolate and to religious administrators and tutors.
2. *Bunreacht na hÉireann, art. 5.*
3. I refer you to an edition of *Studies*, Spring/Summer 1978 devoted to the topic 'Pluralism in Ireland'. There is, among others, an article on 'Constitutional Aspects of Pluralism' by Mary Redmond, Lecturer in Law at U.C.D., a philosophical contribution on 'Principles of Pluralism?' by Frank Dorr of U.C.C., and a theological contribution by Fr Gabriel Daly, O.S.A. entitled 'Christian Response to Religious Pluralism'. This discussion follows a famous debate in Britain, the 'Hart-Devlin' debate, concerned with the enforcement of morals by way of criminal law. It followed the Wolfenden Report (1957). H. L. A. Hart's position is argued in *Law, Liberty, and Morality,* Oxford University Press, 1969, while Devlin's classic is *The Enforcement of Morals,* Oxford University Press, 1965.

diversity and that it is a positive right rooted in the dignity of the human person.

In a pluralist State, the Constitution, while reflecting the spirit, attitudes and common consciousness of the people who evolved it, guarantees to protect in its laws, the basic human *rights* of the citizens (to life, equality before the law, property, good name, etc.). The Constitution can also *evolve,* in the sense that it can be amended by referendum (arts. 46, 47) when a new situation arises which seems to warrant the change. So, for example, in 1972, art. 44.1, of our Constitution was amended, removing the special position originally accorded to 'the Holy Catholic Apostolic and Roman Church as the guardian of the Faith professed by the great majority of the citizens'. This is a reflection of the society's growing maturity, in the sense of a greater awareness of the need to have a clear expression of *respect* for other denominations; although one of our legislators, Dr Fitzgerald, said five years ago:

> In the Republic itself the concept of a pluralist society has yet to strike deep roots at a popular level; for many people the idea is an abstract rather than an intellectual *(sic)* one, at variance with a traditional inherited value system which for historical reasons has not had occasion in the past to distinguish clearly between religious and secular loyalties.[4]

The initiative to alter the Constitution may come from the legislators themselves or from groups within the State. It may also come from the pressures of belonging to the European Community. Equality of pay for women came from our membership of the E.E.C. At Strasbourg, for example, the model adopted by the European Convention on Human Rights and Fundamental Freedoms (to which Ireland is a signatory) is one of pluralism and tolerance. And it was in response to Strasbourg, for example, that Ireland finally abolished corporal punishment in the schools. Human rights evolve, usually through struggle: the right to self-determination was born in revolution. The French Revolution was a struggle for liberty, equality and fraternity. There was the American Revolution and the struggle to abolish slavery and racial discrimination. It was a struggle to gain universal suffrage, and the right of the rising industrial proletariate to strike. The struggle for rights still goes on. The *Universal Declaration of Human Rights* (Dec. 1948) and other international treaties are

4. *Irish Times,* 17 March 1977.

vehicles whereby peoples and nations can attain more rights — social, economic, civil and political rights. Ireland has signed and is committed to implementing many of these international covenants. So, it becomes increasingly pluralist.

Our decision to join the E.E.C. Made us part of a European family of about 250 million people. It will certainly affect our *ethos* in time. We are going to be educated by the process; and that will reflect itself in our future legislation.

LAW IN OUR PLURALIST STATE

It is one thing to deal with moral questions on a personal or inter-personal level, it is quite another to deal with the *legal* aspect of some issues in the domain of public morality. We are concerned here only with the area of *the State's legislation about moral issues in the medical sphere.* And it is here precisely that pluralism, in the sense of respecting the differing sincerely held moral beliefs and convictions, must be fostered and upheld. The laws of a pluralist State like ours have to reflect and respect moral beliefs and considered moral values of different persuasions.

In the judgement handed down by the Supreme Court in the case of *McGee v. The Attorney General* in 1973, Mr Justice Brian Walsh, interpreting the *Constitution* (Article 44), states explicitly that the *Constitution of Ireland* acknowledges that 'religiously speaking, the society we live in is a pluralist one'.[5] Guarantees of religious freedom and freedom of conscience are not confined to the different Christian denominations but extend to the Jewish community, indeed to all citizens. The *Constitution* reads:

> *'Article 44, 2, 10. Freedom of conscience and the free profession and practice of religion are, subject to public order and public morality, guaranteed to every citizen'.*

What we have in the Irish Republic under the *Constitution*, therefore, is a *religious pluralism* (and possibly an ethical pluralism), as distinct from an ideological one.

Furthermore, the general provision of Art. 40.I, which embodies the equal protection clause — *'All citizens shall, as human persons, be held equal before the Law'* — allows the courts to move our society in a progressively pluralist direction, e.g. against all forms of

5. [1974] I.R. 284 at 317.

discrimination. It could be argued that they have been slow to do so but that is scarcely the fault of the law as it stands. It rests finally with the judge to interpret the Constitution.

One of the questions we, as citizens of this pluralist State, must ask ourselves is: are we prepared to grant to others the same freedom of thinking, believing and exercising their religious and moral convictions as we Catholics enjoy in this State?

LAW, MORALITY AND MEDICINE

Moral decisions are being made daily in medical practice. Doctors and nurses deal with birth, suffering and death. Some may be life and death decisions. The moral decisions are often implicit, part of an accepted *ethical code* in the hospital, or part of the practitioner's and patient's religious *belief*. With unprecedented developments in medical science, as well as a growing awareness of a certain pluralism, these implicit moral decisions have had to become explicit; and some are open to question. It is difficult for the doctor or nurse, however highly qualified in medicine, to critically assess the moral situation, or even to know what the precise factors are to be taken into account in arriving at a moral judgement. They need to consult with those competent in moral matters; and together they may reach a responsible and workable solution.

There is a distinction to be made between Moral Theology and Medical Ethics (a part of Moral Philosophy dealing with medical questions); and an ethical *code* (i.e. a code of professional behaviour), alaborated by the medical profession containing definite norms, to act as a guide.[6] This is distinct from State legislation.

Moral Theology derives its moral norms from an authoritative teaching on moral questions from a religious source, e.g. the *magisterium* of the Catholic Church. However, those who are aware of what is going on in the Catholic Church in the post-Vatican II era

6. The Hippocratic Oath, for example, has survived for over 2,400 years. Generations of doctors have made it their programme and pledge. In many Universities today medical graduates still take the Hippocratic Oath in its historical form, changing only the words 'Apollo' and 'Aesculapius' for the word 'God'. A greater number of universities now use the *Geneva Declaration* approved by the World Medical Association (Sept. 1948) which is based on the historical text. This *Declaration* contains the following pledges:
'I will not permit considerations of religion, nationality, race, party politics or social standing to intervene between my duty and my patient.
I will maintain the utmost respect for human life, from the time of conception . . .'.

realise that Catholic theologians and moralists are no longer a monolithic block. The need to update and revise doctrinal teachings, the need for dialogue with modern culture and the new insights of medical science force us to reconsider closely a number of questions on which we have been narrowly dogmatic in the past, treating all moral directives of the Church as equally irreformable. The 1971 Synod of Bishops (Rome) in its statement *Justice in the World* is worth quoting here:

> 'The Church recognises everyone's right to suitable freedom of expression and thought. This includes the right of everyone to be heard in a spirit of dialogue which preserves a *legitimate diversity within the Church'*. (p. 18)

That legitimate diversity or pluralism within the Church raises a problem about *our* attitude to those whose opinions differ from ours. Is it open or closed?

We must also recognise that *different religious traditions* promote different moral norms, which reflect different life-styles and sets of beliefs. So, there are 'Moral Theologies' in the plural. A serious difficulty arises for pluralism when one religious group believes that its own teaching in moral matters is *infallibly* true. It accepts its moral guidance from a religious authority on *faith*. This does not cause undue difficulty when the moral issue is a personal one which does not significantly affect the interests or welfare of others. But it must be tempered by an awareness of religious freedom and freedom of conscience when it comes to imposing moral norms on others in the community without their consent. We need to be particularly vigilant about this in a State which, while professing religious pluralism, may well be 'Confessional' in practice, by imposing the majority Faith's moral belief (e.g. through a referendum) because of a guaranteed voting majority in the electorate. This is a serious and complex issue for any democratic State, but more so for us, where the distinct danger exists of exercising *moral and religious imperialism,* on the paternalistic principle that 'we know best; we have it on divine authority'!

The Irish Catholic Bishops' Conference (14-16 June, 1976) issued a statement on the question of public morality and felt it necessary to point out that:

> 'it is not the view of the Catholic hierarchy, that, in the law of the State, "the principles peculiar to *our* faith should be made

binding on people who do not adhere to that faith' ... the question to be decided in matters of this kind — as far as State law is concerned — is the *impact on society* which a change in the law would be likely to have'.[7]

Obviously the Church has a right to express its own views on such issues of public morality as contraception, divorce, sterilization and abortion. It has a right to teach and defend these views; and, indeed, to incorporate them into policy decisions governing Catholic private hospitals. The burning issue is the case of policy decisions governing State hospitals and publicly funded hospitals, Voluntary Hospitals; and even there — as the Conference of Bishops points out — the conscientious rights of believers must not be infringed.[8] So, for example, we could assume, *prima facie* at least, the right of people with religious objections to voluntary sterilization (e.g. tubal ligation) to refuse to co-operate in such procedures, even in non-religious hospitals.[9] On the other hand, to *prohibit* the provision of hospital

7. News Release from the Catholic Press and Information Office (A Commission of the Irish Bishops' Conference), June 1976. The same statement, which has to do mainly with the *divorce* issue, goes on to say that 'Questions such as these — on the likely effect on society of a change in State law — are obviously open to public debate and yet they are the questions which are usually avoided.' In a similar statement (November 1973) made in the context of proposals to change the law on the sale of *contraceptives,* having again stressed the adverse social consequences of the proposed change, the Bishops' Conference says: 'We emphasise that it is not a matter for bishops to decide whether the law should be changed or not. That is a matter for the legislators, after a conscientious consideration of all the factors involved'. Consistently with that a Statement of April 4, 1978 (n.5) says: 'The matters to which we shall refer are, all of them, questions of public morality. They are concerned with the impact on society which certain changes in legislation would be likely to have'.
8. Cf. Statement from the Catholic Bishops' Conference on proposed legislation dealing with Family Planning and Contraception, 4 April 1978, n. II.
9. I say *'prima facie',* because other factors affecting the health of a patient could enter into the situation, if, for example, most of the staff available were 'conscientious objectors'! Furthermore, the moral teaching of the Catholic Church on voluntary sterilisation is not as clear-cut as some members of the medical profession or the Pro-Life Amendment Campaign claim. I refer you, for example, to a book published ten years ago, *Medical Ethics* (St Paul Publications: Slough, England, 1972) published by the Catholic moral theologian, Fr Bernard Häring (a book, incidentally, bearing an *Imprimatur and Nihil Obstat)* pp. 90-91, where he says:
'But wherever the direct preoccupation is responsible care for the health of persons or for saving marriage ..., sterilization can then receive its justification from valid medical reasons. If, therefore, a competent physician can determine, in full agreement with his patient, that in this particular situation a new pregnancy must be excluded now and forever because it

facilities for *therapeutic* voluntary sterilization in publicly funded hospitals is to impose the views imputed to one religious denomination on public hospitals, in whatever way that is achieved. And that is a failure to respect the pluralist nature of the State.

The role of the moral theologian is to act as a mediator between, on the one hand, his own Church's moral teaching and the medical practitioners of his persuasion who want to inform their conscience and who, in turn, can inform him of new developments and creative tensions which arise in the field of medicine. The exchange involved in such self-reflection and interdisciplinary dialogue ensures Theology's contribution to Medical Ethics. In practice, here in Ireland, this exercise in theological ethics or the Medical Ethics of the Church itself, is commonly referred to as 'Medical Ethics'.

In the strict sense of the term, however, Medical Ethics falls within the domain of philosophical reflection. But, obviously, such reflection cannot divorce itself from the *ethos* of the society — a broadly Christian *ethos* in this case — also the ethical code of the medical profession, the contributions of the sciences (natural and human), but in particular medical science, as well as the moral beliefs of the citizens. Otherwise, it would be forced to operate in a vacuum. Such a philosophical reflection should try to integrate the contributions of all relevant sciences in constructing a coherent moral and political theory which will form the basis for legislation in these matters.

II. — ANTI-ABORTION LEGISLATION

Let me focus on one very topical issue in Ireland, one which shows all the complexities involved in questions of law and public morality. The

---

would be thoroughly irresponsible, and if from a medical point of view sterilization is the best possible solution, it cannot be against the principles of medical ethics, nor is it against 'natural law' *(recta ratio)*. (p. 90)

Häring gives an example of a situation in which sterilization would be permissible:

'If, for instance, the last two pregnancies of this woman have triggered a psychosis and there is no hope that her husband will act responsibly, tubal ligation may be the only or at least the best means of saving the mother for the fulfilment of her task as wife and mother in her already trying situation. There are many other cases of comparable gravity. There are situations where the easier and more just solution would demand the sterilization of the [inconsiderate] husband . . .'

This discerning position about therapeutic sterilization is repeated in Häring's recent three-volume work on Moral Theology, *Free and Faithful in Christ*, Vol. 3, pp. 20-21.

example falls squarely in the field of Medical Ethics. I'm referring to the efforts being made to introduce some kind of anti-abortion law reform; and in particular the 'Pro-Life Amendment Campaign' whose purpose is to bring about an amendment to the *Constitution* which would protect the life of the unborn child from the moment of conception. That is a clear case of the meeting of Law and Morality. And the Taoiseach has promised to introduce an appropriate Bill to the Dáil to this effect before the end of the year.

The present law, under which abortion is illegal in this country, dates back to the 'Offences Against the Person Act' of 1861. It was an Act of the United Kingdom Parliament. No subsequent legislation has been introduced here in Ireland about abortion. The language of the Act is quaint and archaic; so I refrain from quoting it *verbatim*. Section 58 of this 'Offences Against the Persons Act' states, in brief, that it is an offence if one 'unlawfully' does anything to procure a miscarriage. In other words, the 'unlawful', deliberate or induced expulsion of a living, non-viable foetus from the mother's womb is a felony or criminal offence; and it is punishable by imprisonment for life or for any shorter term.[10]

The precise scope or interpretation of this law has never been pronounced upon by an Irish court. The barrister, Mr William Binchy (Member of the Law Reform Commission) claimed recently in the *Irish Medical Times* (March 10, 1978) that it is *probable* that an abortion would be deemed legally permissible in a case where this was medically judged to be the only course open to save the mother from certain death. Beyond that, Binchy claims, 'one enters a grey area where the possibility of a successful (legal) defence becomes progressively less assured. Only a judicial decision can clarify the position'.[11]

It would need to be decided in the Courts what precisely is meant in the Act by *'unlawfully'* procuring a miscarriage. The law seems to imply that there are 'lawful' means of procuring an abortion! In fact, an interesting test case brought to the courts in England (1939) against the surgeon Dr Alex Bourne under that same 1861 'Offences Against the Persons Act' was the case of a 13-year old girl raped by four soldiers and found to be pregnant. The court acquitted the surgeon who performed the abortion. In other words, the *abortion* after rape was *not* considered in this case to be an 'unlawful' procuring of a

10. 'Offences Against the Person Act', 1861, Sect. 58 (24 & 25 Vict., c. 100). Procuring or supplying drugs or instruments with intent to cause an abortion is made an offence by section 59 of the Act.
11. William Binchy, 'Abortion and the Law as it applies in Ireland Today', in *Irish Medical Times*, March 10, 1978, p. 16.

miscarriage. It was deemed by the jury to have been legally perm s-
sible. In England the Abortion Act 1967 superseded all previous
legislation on the matter; but the Offences Against the Person Act,
1861, is still the only law that makes abortion illegal here in Ireland.
The position is that, under the prevailing circumstances, the same
kind of situation could arise here. This Act could be challenged in the
courts as being unconstitutional. (Senator Mary Robinson considers
that it cannot; that Supreme Court judgements by Mr Justice Walsh
in the McGee case, 1974, and in an adoption case in 1979 stipulate
that the right of the unborn child to life *is* already sufficiently protected. William Binchy of the Association of Lawyers for the Defence
of the Unborn, says this is not so, that Mr Justice Brian Walsh was a
'lone voice' in the Supreme Court when he suggested this; and that
his remarks were not binding. They were *obiter dicta*. So, lawyers as
well as doctors differ).

The right to life of the unborn child, I would argue, needs more
legal protection than is presently accorded to it. The law is uncertain
and has not developed. I say this particularly in the light of the
American situation, which, like our own, has a written Constitution
without explicit reference to the rights of the unborn child. And in
1973 the United States Supereme Court recognised the right to
abortion on the grounds that unborn children were not 'persons'; and
that during the first three months the State should not interfere with
the *private* decision to abort reached by a woman and her physician,
exercising his medical judgement. If that can happen in the United
States in the 1970's, it could happen in Ireland in the late 1980's or
1990's.

The question remains, however, as to how best to protect the right
of the unborn, *legally,* without at the same time making of it such an
absolute or 'antecedent' right that it would admit of no exceptions,
even in extreme and specified cases; and to ensure that the right of the
unborn would not be such as to supersede the already guaranteed personal rights of the citizens (*Constitution,* art. 40, sect. 3). We mu'
remember that even in this State where respect for life is an abso' ⌄
priority and the cornerstone of our society, the general prohibition
'Thou shalt not kill' admits of exceptions, e.g. in the case of self-
defence (within drastic limits), war, and the somewhat debatable case
of capital punishment, still accepted in this country, though not in
Britain (except in the case of high treason and certain military
offences). It would be foolhardy to assume as our starting-point that
the general prohibition *'Thou shalt not abort a non-viable living
foetus'* would admit of no exceptions.

I say this with full personal conviction of the sacred character and value of human life. I repeat, I am staunchly *anti-abortionist*. I have an unconditional respect for human life; so that any exceptions to the law that I would advocate would not be *anti*-life; they would not be instances of a direct choice against life, but always open to the value of life. My own, firmly held, personal *moral* position on abortion is in line with the Catholic Church's teaching. Vatican II in its Pastoral Constitution on 'The Church in the Modern World' (*Gaudium et Spes*, n. 51) passes a severe judgement on abortion:

> '. . . from the moment of its conception life must be protected with the greatest care, while abortion and infanticide are unspeakable crimes'.

There is an anti-abortion tradition, differing in details, but going back to apostolic times which has equated abortion with homicide, sometimes with parricide.[12]

My concern, therefore, is certainly *not* to make abortion more readily available or to provide legal loopholes for indiscriminate abortion requests. I am concerned as any other to curtail, in a responsible way, sex consumerism in our society. I am prepared to throw a critical eye on the precise *moral malice* of abortion and to ask whether the same malice is ascribable to all cases; but that is not the precise question before us.

We have to distinguish between the *medical,* the *legal* and the *moral* aspects of abortion. My purpose is to think through the grave difficulties that legislators, moralists and medical personnel face in devising a just and humane abortion law, a law which will protect the rights of both mother and foetus; and which at the same time will not place us on the much dreaded 'slippery slope' of abortion-on-demand which undermines respect and reverence for life in the community. This is a realistic and well-founded fear in the minds of many conscientious people in Ireland today. Granted, it is not a moral argument. But if that fear bids us 'leave well alone', then that may turn our to be the rock on which Irish society will perish. It may not be possible to 'copper-fasten' an anti-abortion law; but it does seem timely to revise the law, introducing an overall prohibition on abortion and permitting some very specific legal exceptions within the general law. Such a law would not derogate from respect for human

12. Cf. John T. Noonan, Jr., 'An Almost Absolute Value in History', in *The Morality of Abortion,* (ed. John T. Noonan, Jr.), Cambridge, Mass., 19.

life, but would face squarely the problem of the genuine conflict of allegedly *equal* human rights. I say 'allegedly' because, was it not St Thomas Aquinas who said that *'. . . one is more strictly bound to make provision for one's own life than to make provision for the life of another'?* (S. Th. II-II, q. 64, a.7).[13] He was arguing in the not totally unrelated context of the right to self-defence, one of the accepted exceptions to the general prohibition 'Thou shalt not kill'.

The three cases most commonly cited in our culture as sufficiently grave to be considered exceptions to the general prohibitions on abortion are the following:

1. Where a pregnancy poses a serious/grave and imminent threat to the *life of the mother.*
2. When a woman has conceived as a result of *rape.* (Sometimes *incest* is included in this exception, but for essentially different reasons).[14]
3. When the foetus is known to be so seriously deformed that it does not have the necessary anatomical structure to develop into or survive as a conscious human being (e.g. a foetus that develops without a brain structure, the *anencephalic* foetus, and is removed in order to prevent grave damage to the mother's psychological health).[15]

I am not saying that all three are accepted by the Catholic Church. N.I is accepted in certain well-defined cases on the basis of the 'principle of double effect'. No.2 is not, as far as I know, accepted by Catholic theologians generally. N.3 is proposed as a 'probable opinion' by some Catholic theologians and is more generally held by Protestant theologians and moralists.

My primary concern here is not to argue the *moral* grounds for the acceptance or rejection of these proposed exceptions, but rather to consider the position of the legislature of a pluralist State confronted with the task of introducing a general legal prohibition about a moral issue, admitting of a range of exceptions, some more widely accepted than others and derived from different sources.

13. *S. Th.* II-II, q. 64, a.7: 'Nec est necessarium ad salutem ut homo actum moderate tutelae praetermittat ad evitandum occisionem alterius; *quia plus tenetur homo vitae suae providere quam vitae alienae.'*
14. See, for example, John Powell, S.J., *Abortion: The Silent Holocaust,* Argus Communications, Texas, 1981, p. 121.
15. Cf. Bernard Häring, *Free and Faithful in Christ. Moral Theology for Priests and laity,* Vol III — 'Light to the World. Salt for the Earth', St Paul Publications, Slough, 1981, p. 34.

III. – 'PRO-LIFE AMENDMENT CAMPAIGN'

Let me say a word about the self-styled 'Pro-Life Amendment Campaign'. Its proponents are urging that the Constitution be amended to guarantee the *absolute* right to life of the foetus or unborn child from the moment of conception. I do not question the integrity or sincerity or purpose of its proponents. I accept it as a sincere effort on their part to prevent, by Constitutional amendment, any future change in legislation which would move away from the present legal prohibition on abortion, presumably because some woman might challenge the 1861 'Offences Against the Person Act' in the courts and win, thereby forcing the legislature to change the law on abortion. Only a Constitutional guarantee, they claim, could stop that happening, and in that way avoid what is now commonly referred to as the 'slippery slope' toward 'abortion-on-demand' or the 'abortion mentality'.

While such a stand is commendable in its respect for life; and while I would wholeheartedly accept and support a broader-based 'pro-life ethic' as a basis for legislation, (rather than, for example, a utilitarian, or pragmatic, or 'quality of life' ethic), some questions have to be raised about the Pro-Life's present campaign to amend the Constitution and so to change the legal position on abortion in Ireland. This is the *legal* rather than the moral aspect of the question. The two cannot be entirely separated; but what is being demanded, I contend, is a *constitutional* change based on a particular moral belief or conviction.

1. THE NAME, 'PRO-LIFE'

First, the name 'Pro-Life', which the group has chosen to call its campaign, implicitly suggests that anyone — like me — who disagrees with its particular proposals, for various reasons which I'll explain, is *anti*-life. This is a false implication. Furthermore, the 'Pro-Life' position at issue argues rather *selectively* for the absolute right-to-life of the unborn child, ignoring the lack of rights of the illegitimate child under the present law, as well as the crucial conflict with another right-to-life, namely, the right-to-life of the mother of that foetus. The 'Pro-Life Amendment Campaign' does not make it sufficiently clear how, under the proposed amendment, a pregnant woman and her physician could take appropriate action to save her life in the case of a serious and imminent threat to her life by the presence of the foetus.

And it is simply not true to say that such a genuine conflict of rights to life *could* not occur in the present state of medical progress. Medical facilities are not the same everywhere. Fortunately, these situations are becoming increasingly rare with advances in medical research and prenatal care. The rarity of such cases, however, does not weaken the validity of this exception to a general prohibition on abortion.

2. PRINCIPLE OF DOUBLE EFFECT

The position of the 'Pro-Life' movement regarding its proposed Constitutional amendment is not quite as clear-cut as it might first appear. It claims that doctors could, in fact, decide to take the necessary measures to save a woman's life, if, for example, her life were threatened by a ruptured ectopic pregnancy (in which case the foetus is not viable); or in the case of early diagnosed malignant cancer of the uterus. Pro-Life members defend this position by appealing to the traditional moral principle known as 'the principle of double effect'. In using this principle, the claim is that *the good effect directly intended* by the doctor is to remove a pathological condition, thereby saving the mother's life; while *the secondary evil effect* — the death of the foetus — is an indirect consequence which is merely 'permitted', 'indirectly foreseen', etc. The argument is that the evil effect is not part of the direct or primary intention, which is, to save the mother's life. This 'principle of double effect' is a standard, traditional Roman Catholic defence of 'indirect abortion'. The 'Pro-Life Amendment Camapign' claims that the death of the foetus in this case is not an 'exception' to abortion, but rather that it is not 'abortion'. (Incidentally, this principle of double effect has been disputed for centuries, even within the Catholic Church, because of the ambiguity and apparent sleight of hand involved in arguing about what is 'directly intended' and what is 'indirectly foreseen' and 'permitted'). There is a moment of choice involved relating to the life of the foetus. It is sheer casuistry to attempt to deny it. But the central point at issue here is that in the life-saving 'indirect abortion' operation (or whatever one now chooses to call it) there is no direct choice against life involved. If, for example, an artificial womb or restorative operation were available for the aborted foetus, the mother and doctor would presumably wish to make these available to the foetus. This hypothetical case simply indicates where the 'direct intention' lies,[16] or what the

16. Cf. Germain Grisez, *Abortion: the Myths, the Realities and the Arguments,* New York, 1970, p. 341; also in 'Toward a Consistent Natural-Law Ethics of Killing', in *American Journal of Jurisprudence,* Vol. 15 (1970), p. 95.

dominant motive was for acting in this way. In other words, it shows it *not* to be an anti-life choice. But there is no point in pretending to ourselves that there is *no* intention regarding the death of the foetus in performing a hysterectomy so as to remove the cancerous womb of a pregnant woman. Or do I fail to see a distinction between 'letting the unborn child die', by removing its life-sustaining environment, and 'killing the child'?

I would argue that this so-called 'indirect abortion' should be an exception to the general law. Doctors cannot know for certain whether this is the 'unlawful' procuring of a miscarriage under the present law, unless it is enshrined in the new legislation or else tried in the courts. It is not enough for the Pro-Life people to say: 'Well! This is not an abortion'. Who has decided on that particular use of language? The medical definition of abortion is the termination of pregnancy before twenty-eight weeks.

3. TWO 'EXCEPTIONS'

While the 'Pro-Life Amendment' proponents want, on the one hand, a Constitutional amendment guaranteeing the right to life of the unborn child, they also want to allow for two 'exceptions', namely, the two cases already referred to in regard to saving the mother's life, but they do not want to concede that they are exceptions to a general prohibition on abortion. Whether they choose to call them exceptions or not, the proponents are specifying what *they* have decided are the permissible parameters of abortion; and they 'happen' to coincide with those very exceptions traditionally recognised by the Catholic Church. Nevertheless, they claim to be 'non-sectarian' in their membership and intentions. Now, since the Irish Constitution is deemed to be pluralist, religiously speaking, I cannot see how the law could stipulate only those exceptions endorsed by the Catholic Church. It is difficult to see why one should justify these specific life-threatening situations *only,* rather than argue for *the legal provision for therapeutic abortion in a medically judged life-threatening condition of the pregnant woman.* Other life-threatening situations may conceivably arise which would not then be covered by the law. What is the doctor to do then?

In fact, in the 'Ethical Code for Hospitals' in the Archdiocese of Dublin, currently in use as a general guideline for resolving some ethical issues which arise in hospitals and taking its inspiration from the Judaeo-Christian ethic, we read:

'Operations and treatment necessary for the care of serious organic pathological conditions of the mother, which cannot be postponed until the foetus is viable, are permitted even though the death of the foetus results. This principle applies also to extrauterine pregnancies'.

If the 'Pro-Life Amendment Campaign' retrenches its position so as to deny the scope for any such exceptions which would protect the mother's life, advocating an absolute ('copper-fastened') prohibition on abortion under any circumstances, it will then have to justify a moral position which accords all rights of protection to the life of the foetus and none to the pregnant woman! This, I contend, would be both constitutionally and morally unacceptable.

4. IMPAIRMENT OF HEALTH

So far, I have referred only to *life*-threatening situations. But there are many Protestant theologians who would justify an interruption of pregnancy, at least *in the very early stages,* where otherwise the *health* of the mother would be permanently and gravely *impaired*. And, while I personally would not find their reasons convincing, I would find it very difficult to justify my opposition to the *legislation* of a pluralist State which would allow freedom in such cases to the physicians and the mothers to decide according to their consciences. As the Catholic moral theologian, Fr Bernard Häring, points out in this regard: 'We should remember that for centuries, Catholic theologians and doctors had the same convictions, based on the opinion that in the early stages of pregnancy we are not yet faced with a human person in the full sense'.[17] Some people are still genuinely convinced that there is scope for argument about when the right to life begins. The 'Pro-Life Amendment Campaign' explicitly states its belief that it is 'from the moment of conception'. So does the Catholic Church.

Modern science is sometimes quoted to back up this position, that is, to confirm the view that a human life-form is present from the moment of conception. What is true is that the genetic make-up of the child is determined from the moment of conception (with the exception of the possible splitting up, which accounts for twins). Genetic material is alreay determined at that early stage; and in that broad sense the foetus has a human (as opposed to a canine) life-

17. *Op. cit.,* p. 34.

form. There is no general disagreement on that. But let us not confuse that with saying that we then have a human person, susceptible
of rights. We cannot simply collapse that distinction between some
kind of human life-form and a human person so as to slide over *the
real source of disagreement*. Science does not and cannot decide what
constitutes a human person. It can pronounce only that this creature
is genetically human. But who is to decide when this early cellular
configuration becomes a person with equal human rights? In other
areas of medical science, in reating of the moment of death, for
example, the presence or absence of brain activity is centrally important. You lose your citizen rights if you are irreversibly brain-dead!
What then of the alleged rights to be accorded to a foetus which has
not yet developed a brain-structure? The legal or moral status of the
foetus in its early stages (6 to 8 weeks) is not clearly established. That
is the way the argument runs.

While personally subscribing to the Catholic view, and accepting
the findings of modern science about the presence of a human life-
form from the moment of conception, I think the question must still
be raised about providing in our legislation for such an exception as
long as there remain upright convictions and well-grounded doubts as
to the precise moment of the 'beginning of human life', in the sense of
a person, who can assume or be given 'rights'. It makes a great
difference to one's moral judgement on conflicting rights to life
whether one regards the foetus as a human being, having the status of
a person, or only a tissue or newly implanted clump of cells *on the
way* to becoming a human being. As long as this question is not
'settled', what does the 'Pro-Life Amendment Campaign' propose to
our legislators? Are we to vote to impose the views of the majority religion?

5. ABORTION AFTER RAPE

Again, in legislating for a pluralist State, in the sense defined, there is
one highly controversial exception which should be faced — that is,
pregnancy as a result of *forcible rape* as grounds for abortion in the
law. It is not an exception that is accepted by Catholic theologians.
But there are nevertheless, many Christians of other denominations
who would regard it as morally justifiable to abort the foetus as soon
as possible after rape.[18] Emotional considerations should not prevent

18. In a sermon delivered in the chapel of the Rotunda Hospital, Dublin, 22 March
1981, the Most Reverend H. R. McAdoo, the Church of Ireland Archbishop of

us from at least *considering* the case of rape. We should also exercise extreme compassion towards a genuine rape victim and appreciate the traumatic experience of a girl brutally assaulted and conceiving the child of such an abhorrent assailant against her will.[19] Moralists will argue that lack of consent is an important moral ingredient here, as is the right of the mother to decide what happens in and to her body, although these are not necessarily the only, or even the over-riding considerations to be taken into account.

On the *Catholic Church's* view, once conception has occurred, then the right to life of the foetus becomes paramount. The human foetus is to be given the same consideration as other human beings; and the only conflicting right to be considered (morally) is that of the threatened life of the mother, if such a threat exists in the particular case. The *foetus* is not regarded as an unjust aggressor but an innocent human being. The woman's integrity has been seriously violated, not by the foetus but by the rapist. The appeal of some contemporary moralists to the right of the woman to decide what will happen in and to her body needs to be carefully interpreted, because once impregnation has occurred, her decision to abort is (on the Catholic view) a decision about what will happen to another person's body, the unborn child's body! Catholic moral teaching maintains that the mother, once pregnant, assumes certain duties towards the unborn child, in particular to protect its life till birth. We sometimes have to suffer the consequences of behaviour which we in no way intended. To have the unborn baby aborted does not help the baby. In the short term it may well relieve the mother of a traumatic burden; but it may also leave her with a lifelong memory of having

---

Dublin, made the following statement on abortion as representing the Anglican posi-tion:

'In the strongest terms, Christians reject the practice of induced abortion, or infanticide, which involved the killing of a life already conceived (as well as a violation of the personality of the mother) *save at the dictate of strict and un-deniable medical necessity'*. He goes on to state that 'some would wish to in-clude under the heading of medical necessity the case of an innocent victim of *rape* whose mental and psychological health and stability would be seriously threatened by having to bear the child conceived'. *(Italics mine)*.

19. Bernard Häring in *Medical Ethics,* p. 115, while not accepting that abortion after rape is objectively morally permissible, states nevertheless: 'I fail to see that a physician can be charged with the malice of abortion if the rape victim cannot be in-duced (motivated) to keep the foetus and if therefore, he is regretfully obliged to ac-cept what, in his eyes, is the best possible solution'. He is referring to a case where the woman has decided that she could not bear the burden of pregnancy, she is near despair, and is in invincible ignorance about the morality of the act.

once carried a child which she had chosen to destroy. Today's experience is tomorrow's memory. And, generally, the experience of abortion is even more traumatic than that of rape, because it is a long, painful and haunting memory, which causes extreme psychological distress. These are some of the reasons why Catholics would not accept abortion after rape as *morally* permissible for them.

Christians of other denominations and non-Christian humanist moralists argue that in the case where pregnancy has been *carefully judged to be the result of rape,* there is a genuine and difficult conflict of rights between two innocent human beings, the mother and the foetus. On this view, what is questioned is how and why the mother can contract moral obligations under coercion. Morality being the domain of personal freedom and responsibility, it is difficult to evolve a moral theory which would require the mother to contract a moral obligation without her consent. Some striking hypothetical analogies have been provided by moralists.[20]

If legal abortions were to be sought on the grounds of rape, it would be imperative to require that a report of rape be formally lodged with the police authorities and that medical examination and care be given immediately after the rape incident. The law would be wide open to abuse if a false appeal to rape were to be used as an excuse for procuring an abortion. Efforts to provide legislation for proper procedures in rape cases are badly needed in Ireland.

This exception to a general prohibition on abortion, while strongly advocated by some moralists, is fraught with difficulties — not only moral difficulties, emotive reactions, but practical questions of establishing the fact of rape. But I may now be engaging in a 'slippery slope' argument. All I would advocate is that the question should get a fair hearing.

20. Judith J. Thompson in an article 'A Defence of Abortion' *(The Philosophy of Law,* edit. by R. M. Dworkin, Oxford Readings in Philosophy, Oxford University Press, 1977, ppl 112-128) tries to defend abortion after rape by drawing an interesting fictitious analogy about conflicting rights with a famous unconscious violinist who has been found to have a fatal kidney ailment, and the Society of Music Lovers, *having tried all other means,* find that you alone have the right blood type to save him. They kidnap you and plug the violinist's circulatory system in yours, so that your kidneys can be used to extract poisons. The violinist is now plugged into you (without your consent). To unplug you would be to kill him. Is it morally incumbent on you to accede to this situation for nine months, or for life?

While this is an interesting hypothetical analogy which helps us to reflect on the implications of clashes in the right-to-life, to my mind it is a defective analogy for reasons which I cannot explain here. *Analogia claudicat!*

6. THE ANENCEPHALIC

We must also ask if the 'Pro-Life Amendment Campaign' takes account of the views of some Catholic moral theologians, like the world-renowned Fr Bernard Häring, and theologians of other Christian denominations who would argue for the *third* exception mentioned (see above). Fr Häring says:

> 'I consider probable the opinion of those who justify the removal of a foetus that surely cannot survive, when the action is taken in order to prevent grave damage to the mother. For instance, an anencephalic foetus not only cannot develop into a conscious human life but cannot survive. To remove it in order to spare great damage to the mother is truly therapeutic, while no injustice is done to the life of this foetus already doomed to death. Traditional moral theology would have called this intervention an "indirect abortion".'[21]

It is difficult to see what is so 'indirect' about such a removal of the foetus. There are two elements in this very specific exception of the anencephalic: *firstly,* the foetus, not having a brain-structure, cannot develop into a conscious post-natal human being; if it is not still-born, it can very rarely survive beyond 30 hours after birth; *secondly,* it is therapeutic and is intended to 'spare great damage' to the mother. It is not stated by Häring, but severe psychological stress to a mother aware of the condition of the foetus would, presumably, fall under the category of 'great damage' in this instance. Jewish Law would also support such an exception.[22]

If I may interject an 'aside' here, which is relevant to the general topic of 'Medical Ethics in a Pluralist State'. It is this: the most sophisticated medical tests for diagnosing foetal deformity are not commonly available in Irish hospitals — allegedly, for ethical reasons, principally that Ireland does not provide for abortion in such cases; and, consequently, there would be little point in providing such

---

21. Häring, *Free and Faithful in Christ,* Vol. III, p. 34.
22. The Chief Rabbi, Dr David Rosen is quoted in the *Dublin Jewish News* (Oct.-Dec. 1981, p. 14) as saying: 'Jewish Law regards foetal life as life, and therefore prohibits its wanton destruction. Nevertheless, although it is a life, it is not the same kind of life as that of the mother, but is subordinate to her. Therefore, if pregnancy is a considered threat (by qualified medical opinion) to the physical and mental health of the mother, *abortion is not only permissible, it is obligatory,* whether the mother wants it or not'.

diagnostic tests. That in itself is difficult to justify, more particularly in the State hospitals of a pluralist State. Furthermore, as medical research progresses, it is becoming increasingly likely that such tests will be used to detect foetal malfunctioning which can be treated therapeutically *in utero*. This would be medically beneficial to the foetus.

7. LEGAL DILEMMA

Another point about the 'Pro-Life Amendment Campaign' is this: I think it presents a real *dilemma* for the legislators.

On the one hand, if one introduces a blanket prohibition on abortion, such that it gives the foetus 'absolute' or 'antecedent' rights, one thereby, in my opinion, makes the Constitution internally inconsistent (accepting that there are genuine cases of the conflicting rights of two innocent people), because Article 40.I, of the Constitution already provides that 'all citizens shall, as *human persons,* be held equal before the law.' Section 3 of the same article states:

> *'1. The State guarantees in its laws to respect, and as far as practicable, by its laws to defend and vindicate the personal rights of the citizen'.*

It is not clear what precisely the range of those 'personal' rights includes; the list in the Constitution is not exhaustive; but it now includes, for example, the important and relevant 'right to bodily integrity' (*Ryan v. Attorney General* [1965] I.R. 292). Article 40, section 3, goes on to specify some of the rights intended:

> *'2. The State shall, in particular, by its law protect as best it may from unjust attack and, in the case of injustice done, vindicate the life, person, good name, and property rights of every citizen'.*

The Constitution already guarantees to protect the right to *life* of all its citizens as human persons, including that of the mother, whose life may now be threatened by the right to life of the foetus. To elevate the right-to-life of the unborn from being an *implied* fundamental right to an express fundamental right does not solve anything, because one is still on a collision course with the right-to-life of the mother, as well as the right to physical and mental health of the mother. That is one horn of the legal dilemma.

On the other hand, if the Constitutional amendment proposed were to allow *exceptions* to be made to the general law prohibiting abortion (without specifying each one), then the ball would be back in the Courts, which is largely what the 'Pro-Life Amendment Campaign' seeks to avoid. One of the aims of the Pro-Life Amendment Campaign is to preclude jurisdiction of the Supreme Court from constitutional interpretation. No amendment to the Constitution could successfully do that where conflicting rights are involved, as in this instance. In that case one of the main thrusts of the campaign would be defeated, even if it achieved a Constitutional amendment. That is the other horn of the dilemma.

Perhaps the most that can be achieved here is to introduce into the *Constitution* some symbolic statement which would indicate that our society unconditionally rejects unjust *direct* abortion of a living, non-viable foetus, defining 'abortion' in some narrow, technical, legal sense which would at least allow for the exceptions sometimes referred to as 'indirect' abortion'. Perhaps, too instead of inserting a 'right to life', the Constitutional amendment should guarantee rather a 'right of the foetus not to be killed directly', because the impropriety of abortion does not follow from the concession of 'rights' to the unborn child under the Constitution.

An alternative course of action for the 'Pro-Life' proponents would have been to canvass for an Act of the *Oireachtas* which would deal with questions surrounding abortion in a more comprehensive fashion, spelling out what the Courts may or may not do. Admittedly, such an Act could be rescinded by a future Act of the *Oireachtas,* but not without considerable difficulty.

8. OVERSIMPLIFICATION

In the staff lounge of the Hastings Centre (Institute of Society, Ethics and the Life Sciences) in New York State, the following text hangs on the wall:

> *'For every human problem, there is a solution that is simple, neat and wrong'.*

What I fear is that a Constitutional amendment, which would simply place a general prohibition on abortion, would give us a solution which would be 'simple, neat and wrong' in the circumstances. Oversimplification is a temptation to which none of us is immune — politicians, doctors, administrators, priests, philosophers, theologians, legislators. In a society where a narrow dogmatism tends to prevail, in practice (if not in theory), we have to beware of unqualified general assertions dressed up as 'matters of principle'. We tend in this State to insist on the absoluteness of moral principles, principally because the vast majority of the people in this part of the island derive their moral *beliefs* from the same source, viz., the Catholic Church's moral teaching based on faith. *When we come to civil law, we can easily tend to carry over that absoluteness* and to couch our moral beliefs in laws that do not take account of the genuinely held moral beliefs and considered moral judgements of others. That is an undesirable form of moral *imperialism,* deriving from a religious imperialism.

Even within the Christian traditions, general moral principles have to be balanced by a feeling for the complex problems that arise when such principles are applied to particular real-life cases. Likewise in law, general principles can be *'tyrannical'*.

8. WHAT WILL IT ACHIEVE?

Finally, I would like to ask the supporters of the Pro-Life Amendment Campaign *what precisely they hope to achieve.* An amendment to the Constitution will not lessen the thousands of abortions per year. The campaign is not — as I understand it — advocating extra- territorial jurisdiction in relation to Irish women having abortions abroad and returning. The proximity of free, 'safe' abortion clinics in Britain makes it quite unrealistic to be concerned *solely* with banning abortion in this country. A constitutional amendment may ensure that it will continue to be awkward to procure an abortion but it will not be effective legislation because it will not be any more preventive than the present law. We cannot wash our hands of the ethical dilemma which this poses.

9. THE SOCIAL CONTEXT

The law governing abortion cannot be talked about in isolation. The reasons why women choose to have abortions as a final option should be discussed realistically. Many 'unwanted pregnancies' come about as a result of ignorance (e.g. about sexuality); others for different social reasons (e.g. from loneliness of girls away from home, and from severe and intolerant pressures operative in our society). According to social workers who work with the unmarried, the single most significant factor in pushing Irish women to terminate their pregnancies is the hostile attitude of those closest to them. A Constitutional amendment will not reduce by one whit the conservatively estimated, official figure of 3,500 Irish women who went to Britain last year (1981) to have an abortion.[23] We are rightly accused of theorizing in 'ivory towers' if we do not work to create a society where those women who have 'unwanted pregnancies' are offered real facilities to enable them to bring their pregnancy to its term (e.g. the money to be expended on having the referendum, £800,000 to a million pounds, would be better spent in providing one decent hostel for unmarried mothers in Dublin); and also to enable those women to keep their child if they so wished.

A genuine *moral* stance on abortion demands that we take active measures to discover and minimize the complex social causes leading to abortion; and that we prevent abortion by providing a more tolerant social climate and proper facilities so that women facing 'unwanted pregnancies' may more easily bring their children into the world. It is critical to the credibility of the 'Pro-Life' campaign that the pregnant woman be cared for and attended to with the same concern and compassion as that accorded to the unborn child. To speak for one and not the other is inconsistent with the basic pro-life ethic, that each and every human life has absolute value.

CONCLUSION

Having placed all those considerations before you I can appreciate that you may find the issue very confused. One of my aims in the paper was precisely to highlight the complexities involved in matters of law and public morality, particularly in the medical field and in a State which is becoming progressively pluralist. Black-and-white solutions are rare. There are many grey areas. We must also bear in mind that there has been an explosion in human knowledge in this century; and progress in medical science is such that it constantly opens up new problems. Such a situation forces us to be open to revising the formulation of our ethical principles from time to time.

Some readers may find it difficult to distinguish between arguments put forward for positions which I personally hold and other reasoned arguments for positions to which I do not subscribe because of a *religiously* informed conscience. That is a risk I must take. I repeat one point, about the morality of abortion, namely, that I

---

23. According to statistics issued by the Office of Population Censuses and Surveys in London, covering the years 1968-Sept. 1981, a conservative estimate of 18,500 Irish women had legal abortions in the U.K.

consider direct abortion, i.e. any deliberate procedure, the direct purpose of which is to prevent the implantation of the foetus or to expel it from the womb before it is viable, to be immoral. It offends against a fundamental human right. I have not addressed myself directly in this paper to that question of the morality of abortion. But I do not wish to give the impression that I have no deep convictions on the matter.

I am satisfied if I have succeeded in opening up a reasonable reflection on the complicated issues involved and in highlighting the difference between the legal and moral aspects of the problem. I can only hope to do so in an atmosphere of post-Vatican II's respect for religious freedom and freedom of conscience. It is a matter of 'historical fact that down to the 1960's a positive response to pluralism was not a live option for Roman Catholics.'[24] The situation has now changed in theory. Let us see if it has done so in practice, allowing a debate on matters of public morality without fear, righteous indignation or acrimony. Let us look at Christ's apprach to others. Coercion of any kind was utterly foreign to him. Let us return to the freedom of the gospel. If love, not fear, recrimination and sanction, is to tule this country, we must have freedom — not only for the majority, but for those who dissent.[25]

POST SCRIPTUM

This paper was written prior to the announcement of the text of the amendment, and was based on what SPUC was proposing in the summer of 1982.

24. Fr Gabriel Daly, 'Christian Response to Religious Pluralism', in *Studies* Spring/Summer 1978, p. 68.
25. This paper was prepared for reading to a particular audience and not as a scientific article for publication. Since I have been asked to publish it in its original form, I cannot supply adequate footnoting, references, etc., as I would like. I must, therefore, acknowledge in general the help given to me by colleagues at U.C.C. and by the Thomas Davis Lecture series (RTE Radio, 1981) 'Morality and the Law. Conflict and Consensus in Irish Society', wherein some of these issues have already been discussed.

Pro-Life Amendment

A critical appraisal of the paper 'Medical Ethics in the Pluralist State'

CONLETH A. BYRNE, O.P.

Some of the reactions to Fr Brendan O'Mahony's contribution alert us to the possible confusion and emotionalism[1] we are likely to work ourselves into about the proposed pro-life amendment to the Constitution, unless we are clear about what exactly we are being asked to decide on. We are *not* being asked to decide whether we are for or against abortion. If that were the issue, there is little doubt that the vast majority of Irish voters today would declare themselves against abortion and pro-life. What we *are* being asked to decide is whether or not this widely held conviction should be embodied in our Constitution, in the form of an amendment, to prevent legislation being passed to legalize abortion in our country.

To my mind Fr O'Mahony was mainly trying to alert us to the problems this proposed amendment gives rise to. First, a blanket ban on abortion, without further qualification or clarification, could be taken to exclude certain practices which the medical profession in Ireland today regards as quite acceptable to protect the life and health of pregnant mothers, like removing a cancerous womb containing a live foetus, or a tube that is damaged by a developing fertilized ovum out of place. It might also preempt discussion of other delicate cases, like allowing a mother to carry to full term a foetus shown clearly to have no brain, or even continuing efforts to produce so-called 'test-tube babies'.

Against this those in favour of the amendment will argue that these special cases can be catered for in the wording of the proposed amendment. As I understand him, Fr O'Mahony was simply pointing out that it will be very difficult to do this without importing into our basic civil law elements that belong, not just to specifically Roman Catholic moral teaching, but a specific piece of casuistry, about which even Roman Catholic moralists today are not all fully agreed, not to speak of moralists from other Christian and non-Christian

---

1. Fr Brendan himself is not altogether quit of the charge of emotionalism. Using emotive terms like 'religious and moral imperialism' and 'tyrannical general principles' (p. 58) detracts from the reasoned tone of this delicate discussion. Other reservations I have about Fr Brendan's paper are expressed mainly in the following footnotes.

denominations.[2] In a society like ours, committed to cater equally for all its citizens, many of whom are not convinced Roman Catholics or even Christians, this should not be done. From this point of view the proposed amendment could be seen as ill-conceived and ill-advised.

To argue that what is involved is an issue of basic human rights, and not of religious conviction and practice, is to miss the point. While there may be general agreement about basic human rights, like the right to life, the interpretation of the nature and extent of these rights, and of how they can best be promoted and protected, can lead to disagreements in detail, coloured by religious or denominational allegiance. Where this happens, one particular point of view should not be imposed on those who do not accept it, unless they are a completely unrepresentative and irresponsible minority.[3]

CONVINCE FUTURE GENERATIONS

The reasons advanced for the proposed amendment are that the right to life of the unborn child is not adequately guaranteed by our Constitution, as it stands, and that the law by which it is presently

2. This is the so-called 'principle of double effect' explained by Fr O'Mahony on p. 50. Though this is *not* an exclusively Roman Catholic principle, it continues to be widely used in the specifically Roman Catholic moral tradition, while other moralists, including some Roman Catholics now, are tending to abandon it in favour of broader principles, like 'proportionality' or 'the lesser evil'. This has to be taken into account in the present amendment debate. Still, the subtlety of 'double effect' reasoning should not be so lightly dismissed as mere 'sleight of hand' (p. 50). It is valid for many cases, though perhaps it conceals an underlying principle or 'proportionality' or 'the lesser evil', from which it maybe draws its real force and validity.

Also it is not quite right to suggest, as Fr O'Mahony seems to do (p. 48), that even 'double effect' moralists regard abortion to save the mother's life as a permitted exception to the general prohibition of abortion (p. 48, n. 1). For them the mother's life would have to be threatened by a pathological condition, the curing of which causes the death of the foetus as an unwanted secondary effect. Hence its destruction is not used as the means of saving its mother's life. This would be excluded by these moralists as 'direct abortion', or 'abortion' in the normal sense in which they use that word. In the permitted case the death of the foetus is simply accepted as the unavoidable consequence of the means that must be used to save its mother's life. Hence it is described as 'indirect' and permissible according to the 'principle of double effect'.

Again Häring (quoted by Fr O'Mahony on p. 56) is certainly wrong to include the removal of an anencephalic foetus from the womb within the traditional category of 'indirect abortion', whatever about its justification otherwise.

3. Here I would like to point to what I see as the greatest weakness in Fr Brendan's treatment of this question. One cannot base firm practical conclusions on the

protected could eventually be challenged and changed. (This law, incidentally, provides for a possible sentence of life-imprisonment for the mother who procures an abortion or 'miscarriage'.) The legal justification of this claim will be examined elsewhere.[4] However, by far the best way to ensure that unborn human life continues to be adequately protected by our laws and institutions is to continue to convince future generations of Irish citizens, to whom future legislators will be answerable, of the unacceptability of abortion. They must be persuaded, as we are, that human life, including unborn human life, is far more precious and important than any consideration of social or financial convenience; that killing the unborn is not an acceptable way of coping with even alleged risks to the mother's health or sanity, which can, in any case, be effectively safeguarded in other ways.[5]

To bequeath a constitutional ban on abortion to future generations, without this conviction, would leave them bound by legal

---

demands of a 'pluralism' whose rightful limits are not precisely defined. The mere fact that some members of a society want or do not disapprove of something is *not*, of itself, sufficient reason for framing or changing the laws of that society to allow or not forbid it. Examples like 'fraternities of friendly rapists or bigamists' within the society carricature this point, but make it nonetheless. There have to be other limiting factors, which I here summarize under the headings 'representative' and 'responsible'. These would need to be teased out further, in terms of the need to balance conflicting recognized rights, for example, like the 'right to life' against the 'right to freedom of conscience'. I am not convinced that Fr Brendan has done this adequately, with his description of 'pluralism' variously as: 'respecting differing sincerely held moral beliefs and convictions'; 'reflecting and respecting moral beliefs and considered moral values of different persuasions'; 'progressively moving against all forms of discrimination'; and 'granting to others the same freedom of thinking, believing and exercising their religious and moral convictions as we Catholics enjoy in this State'. I leave it to another contributor to this collection to make the necessary clarifications.

4. Fr O'Mahony himself makes a fair case for the need to tidy up our legal and constitutional barriers to abortion, admitting that there are good grounds for the fears expressed in certain quarters (pp. 45-46). Still I am not happy with his suggestion of an overall prohibition of abortion with specific exceptions written in (p. 48). These will always be matters for responsible individual judgement in each case. They cannot be legislated for in advance, though the law should not be so tight as to leave no room at all for this exercise of responsible judgements either. Trying to provide for them in advance by specific exceptions in law could, I think immediately put us on the slippery slope we all wish to avoid.

5. Fr O'Mahony says he would find it difficult to justify his opposition to legislation that would allow early abortion ('interruption of pregnancy') for serious health reasons (p. 52). While I sympathise with his difficulty, I confess I do not share it. Such legislation could really put us on the slippery slope towards abortion on demand.

restrictions with which they could not identify through genuine conviction and sympathy. They would then do all in their power to evade and remove these restrictions and this could result in a very damaging and divisive political or church-state wrangle in the future.

It may be easy and politically tempting to bring in an amendment when the popular tide is largely running in its favour. It may not be so easy, nor so politically palatable, in view of electoral risks from large and still powerful minorities, to revise or remove an ill-conceived amendment, even if and when majority opinion may have changed or shifted.

At any rate, this is not the best or most effective way to inculcate and promote sound morals. Christian morality should come from within, from the life of Jesus and his Spirit in us, based on personal conviction and commitment, rather than on imposed legal enactments. So, by all means, let there be a vigorous pro-life and anti-abortion campaign; but let it concentrate its energies more on trying to persuade and convince our people, especially our young people, of the values at stake, and on removing the attitudes and inadequacies in our society that tempt them towards abortion, than on legal expedients of questionable effectiveness and motivation.

ADDITION TO THE CONSTITUTION

Still I would, perhaps, like to go a bit beyond Fr O'Mahony and see could I accommodate those who sincerely believe that, to make our national stance on abortion perfectly clear, an amendment to our Constitution is still called for. I would suggest the following simple addition to Article 40.3 of the Constitution. This section reads already:

1° The State guarantees in its laws to respect, and, as far as practicable, by its laws to defend and vindicate the personal rights of the citizen.

2° The State shall, in particular, by its laws protect as best it may from unjust attack and, in the case of injustice done, vindicate the life, person, good name and property rights of every citizen.

To this could be added a third paragraph reading:

3° The guarantee of the right to life contained in 2° above extends even to unborn children from the first moment of their existence as such.

I would use the word 'existence' rather than 'conception' to avoid enshrining in our Constitution another piece of controverted speculation about whether or not a true human being or child is present from the moment of conception or fertilization. Certainly there is a continuous development towards full humanity from that moment on and all the ingredients for that development are present from that first moment. The life that is present from that moment is 'human', at least in the sense that it can never become anything other than a living human person, unless it is aborted or otherwise obstructed in its development. Also no other stage in this development can be clearly identified as the point at which what up to then would have been a *potential* human being becomes an *actual* human being. Hence, for safety sake at least, we have to assume that this starting point coincides with the moment of conception/fertilization.

This does not prove that it does, in fact. Some very respectable authorities have argued that it does not, among them St Thomas Aquinas, who held for a delay of several weeks. Contrary to what is often claimed, his arguments were based, not just on faulty biology, but on sound metaphysical principles regarding potentiality and actuality (though the time-lapse he suggests — 40 days for a boy-child and 80 for a girl-child — is somewhat arbitrary: cf Summa Theologiae I q.76 a.3 ad 3; q.118 a.2 ad 2). We should not exclude the possibility that further reflection and investigation might bring people back to a somewhat similar position, with possible important consequences for medical practice. This could perhaps be relevant to the treatment of rape-victims, mentioned by Fr O'Mahony, though it has to be admitted that this was not envisaged by even those traditional moralists who held for a certain delay before what they called 'ensoulment'.[6]

Meanwhile all human life in the womb will enjoy the solid protection of our Constitution, amended as suggested above. Only positive and convincing evidence that the life involved is not, or not yet, that of a true human being or child can deprive it of this absolute protection. Only then, as a lesser value than that of a human life in the full sense, might it have to compete for protection with other

6. I would not even suggest abortion legislation to cope with cases of rape. Neither would I like to see the kind of narrowly 'anti-abortion' legislation being passed that might prevent everything possible being done, in good conscience, for the victims of rape, to save them from coming to be actually 'with child' as a result of the attack.

The statement relating to rape that 'Morality being the domain of personal freedom and responsibility, it is difficult to evolve a moral theory which would require the mother to contract a moral obligation without her consent' (p. 55) is presumably an opinion cited by Fr Brendan, rather than his own. We all contract a moral obligation to preserve our own lives without our personal consent to be born!

important human and social values. To want more than this, it seems to me, is to seek a constitutional formula 'copper fastened' against genuine advances in science and enlightenment.[7]

OPPOSED TO ABORTION

Finally, in the interests of completeness and total honesty, I must add the following observations. Apart from whatever tidying up might be needed to meet points already raised by me here, if there were ever a positive move to change our present laws and introduce legalized abortion here as in other countries, I would oppose that move. Even if it were made in the name of 'pluralism', out of regard for some dissenting minorities among us, I could not support it.[8] This may seem inconsistent with what I have been saying up to now. If it is, so be it. I would rather be guilty of inconsistency than of the deaths of innocent victims of legalized abortion. I suppose, to remain quite consistent, I would have to regard those minorities on whose behalf the proposed change in our abortion laws might be advocated as 'unrepresentative and irresponsible'. Those who put innocent human lives at risk are certainly irresponsible. I'm convinced they do not include many of those who, like Fr O'Mahony, have expressed reservations about the proposed pro-life amendment to our Constitution.

This is what makes their position so delicate. On the one hand, they are in danger of being claimed by advocates of legalized abortion. On the other hand, they may be attacked as being pro-abortion by those who are strongly against it. Hence their observations should be treated with the utmost respect and sensitivity. Listen to what they are actually saying, instead of just hearing what you expect them to say the more readily to attack or applaud them. Don't be too quick to bundle them into your own or the opposite camp. They could have a lot to teach us about the real meaning of pluralism and respect for life, and about how these two can best be reconciled in our society.

7. At the same time I would not agree with Fr O'Mahony that making the right to life of the unborn explicit in our Constitution would not solve anything. It would at least give the unborn an equal right to life with everyone else, which cannot be outweighed by lesser rights. How this right can be protected in conflict with another's *equal* right can hardly be a matter for general legislation.
8. See notes 3 and 5 above.

What is Pluralism?

GARRETT BARDEN

In the current debate on an amendment to our constitution 'pluralism' is in the air, but is in danger of being trivialized by champions and opponents alike. It has been suggested that pluralism requires the complete relativization of values or that it requires the implementation of any minority claims whatsoever. I want to argue here that it requires neither of these.

NOT THE SAME AS RELATIVISM

First, pluralism and relativism are not the same. From the every-day point of view the sun rises and sets; from the point of view of astronomy the earth revolves on its own axis and moves in orbit around the sun. We can reconcile the statement that the sun rises and sets with the statement that the earth revolves on its own axis and around the sun only by taking account of the two points of view and if we ask which of the statements is true we must be prepared to compare the points of view. If we are not prepared to compare the points of view we have to say that one statement is true from one point of view and the other from the other point of view. Fundamentally, the relativist holds that points of view are not comparable. For the relativist, points of view are just that; they are neither true nor false.

Moral relativism has the same structure. In a debate on abortion the relativist will discover that there are those who are against abortion and those who would allow it. He will try to discover the opposing points of view. Those opposed to abortion may, for example, adopt the point of view of 'the right to life'; those who would allow abortion may adopt the point of view of 'the woman's right to choose'. The relativist will point out these incompatible viewpoints and will claim that there is nothing further to be said.

Neither position on abortion is the relativist position; the relativist position is that both positions are equal and that once one has reached the level of basic viewpoints there can be no further argument.

There are some practical consequences. First, the relativist may have to choose between basic viewpoints and may find himself* adopting one rather than another for obscure motives from his

*This and cognate forms denote both females and males.

personal history. He will, however, hold that his position is not in the end true but is no more than a presupposition which he takes from his culture and upbringing. The second consequence regards not himself but those who adopt the different viewpoint. Here, however much he may find the opposing viewpoint distasteful, he will not say that it is mistaken.

A great deal more should be said of relativism in moral theory and some of its difficulties pointed out. In the space available it may be better to suggest some of its values as they appear to a non-relativist.

For the relativist a particular moral position, a particular moral viewpoint, is not a matter of argument. What is it a matter of? The theory points to the obscurity of moral feeling, sensibility, tradition, upbringing, personal history, personal choices in difficult situations, friendships, loves, examples, revulsions, delights and so on.

Because relativism holds that moral foundations are not a matter of argument, it may recall just how obscure these foundations are; while a theory which holds that moral foundations are fundamentally arguable may easily slip into the mistaken attitude that they are, precisely because arguable, clear. Many of the contributors to the current debate seem to think of their moral lives as they might think of a geometry with self-evident axioms; they seem to think of their moral positions as positions at which they have arrived almost unaided and with little difficulty; they seem to find it offensive to be reminded that moral positions are places, so to speak, where we find ourselves largely because of our upbringing. For we learn our morality almost as we learn our language.

VALUE DIFFERENCES WITHIN THE COMMUNITY

Pluralism is not founded on the principle that fundamental moral viewpoints are beyond argument but it differs from relativism in yet another respect. Its focus of attention is not on the incompativility of different points of view and different positions but on the value of the presence of such differences within the one community.

There are areas of everyday living where we commonly appreciate and rely upon the variety of interests and views without referring to such everyday appreciation as pluralist. Only when differing interests and views oppose one another is there a problem; and when there is a problem there is a tendency to resolve it as simply (but perhaps also as crudely) as possible. The practical resolution of differences sometimes must be crude, at least in the end, but there are different possible attitudes to the resolution.

Views may oppose one another without either view requiring action, and still there may be a problem. For example, a community in which there is widespread belief in God may find it difficult to tolerate, much less appreciate, the presence of atheism. A community within which there is widespread belief in the merits of socialism may find it hard to tolerate the presence of an opposing view. A society in which there is a welcoming attitude to immigrants of a different race or colour may find it hard to appreciate the presence of other sentiments. A society dedicated to achieving its goals by force may find the presence of a dissident voice unpalatable. I have deliberately chosen contrasting examples to illustrate the covert tendency in each of us to pretend that we appreciate opposed views when what we mean is that we want our own views heard when we are in the less powerful position. A society may include opposing views and the virtue of pluralism may still be absent.

MORE THAN A LIBERAL STANCE

The pluralist appreciates views other than his own. Why? The classic liberal position is expressed in the catch-phrase that 'I disagree with you but defend your right to hold your opinion'. This is not yet pluralism although not opposed to it. This liberal position does not so much positively appreciate opposed opinions as appreciate the freedom within which opposed views are permitted. Within classic liberalism an attempt was made to produce a practical principle of action which would restrict the action of the state to preventing actions which did others harm. But the positive appreciation of opposing views or of the presence of other views is not the main part of the liberal argument although neither opposed to nor utterly absent from it.

The pluralist adds to the liberal that not only is it good that there should be a freedom to express opposed views but that it is good that there should be opposed views. A reason for this appreciation is the very real possibility that one's own views are mistaken or incomplete. Pluralism is not content that opposed views should merely exist side by side in a community; the value of the variety is that each should affect the other. To the believer there is a positive value in atheism in that it is a constant challenge to belief and possibly a guard against anthropomorphism. The believer is tempted to invent an easily assimilable image of God — whether comforting or terrifying — and atheism can often show that this image is not worthy of belief. Contrariwise, atheism may be purified by the presence of belief for atheism, too, is tempted to simple mindedness and infallibilism. Belief may discomfit atheism by insistence on a mystery which atheism denies.

NOT RESTRICTED TO RELIGION

But pluralism is not restricted to religion, and theological examples may give a misleading impression. The pluralist in favour of nuclear power, for example, genuinely appreciates the vigorous presence of his opponents with whom he disagrees, for he recognizes that he can be carried away by the bias of his own interest and enthusiasm and may overlook aspects of the situation to which his opponents draw attention. Similarly, the pluralist opponent of nuclear energy will be glad of the opposition with which he entirely disagrees for he, too, is liable to miss features of the situation which are clear to others.

The socialist economist appreciates the presence of supply-side opponents and vice-versa; the analytic philosopher appreciates the presence of other schools; the conservative appreciates the presence of the reformer. In a debate on abortion the pluralist who repudiates abortion appreciates the presence of opponents while the pluralist who supports the legalization of abortion in some cases is glad of the presence of a vigorous opposition. The pluralist who at the present time in Ireland argues against a change in our Constitution knows that the arguments on the other side have been helpful in bringing him to clarify his position while the pluralist who comes down in favour of an amendment will be glad that his arguments have been tested. Both cannot be correct but neither is infallible.

PLURALISM A RULE-OF-THUMB

Pluralism is, then, not any particular position but an attitude to positions and, most fundamentally, an attitude to argument. Still, positions and attitudes are put into practice. Has pluralism anything to offer in the dilemma of putting conflicting views into practice? Liberalism offered the principle or rule of thumb that nothing should be imposed or forbidden except when harm to others was in question. The rule of thumb cannot act like an axiom in geometry, but it is a fairly good guide and should be kept in mind.

A similar pluralistic principle has been suggested: minority views should be allowed practical expression. As a rule of thumb, as something to be kept in mind this is good; elevated to the status of a principle from which action is to be deduced it is simple minded. It often happens that opposing views cannot be put into practice together — opposing views on the death penalty for instance. But there are other less obvious examples. In Ireland at the present time there are some who favour the introduction of divorce; and others who favour a society within which divorce is impossible. It is not possible to accommodate these opposing views and it is no answer to those who want a society without divorce to tell them that there will be no compulsion on them to divorce.

Furthermore, not all views that clamour for realization are acceptable. People are not infallible and are often not even wise; but they do and must judge what they will in the end accept. Those who oppose capital punishment are unenthusiastic about the suggestion that they should allow it on the grounds that a minority (or even a majority) want it; those who oppose slavery are unimpressed by the demands of those who favour it; opponents of corporal punishment will not reintroduce it because some support it.

Pluralism has no easy solution. It offers no alternative to a careful examination of the situation in all its detail. It does, however, suggest that what has to be taken into account is extremely delicate and complex. It knows that in practical affairs it is rarely if ever possible to deal with one value in isolation from others. It knows the great value — as well as the extreme difficulty — of building a community within which opposing views are mutually appreciated. It knows the constant temptation to impose one's own views and to smother the uncertainties that may arise if one genuinely attends to the views of one's opponents. To clarion calls for the imposition of selected values pluralism will incline to point to other values that are being overlooked.

PLURALISM AN ATTITUDE TO WHAT COMMUNITY IS

Pluralism is not a particular position on any issue but an attitude to a dispute and to what a community is. In most contemporary states there are people of differing views on important issues. The pluralist is not ashamed to be practical; he is not afraid of the value of having these people live together in some harmony and mutual appreciation; he is aware of how the failure to appreciate this value has led to some quite awful results.

In the current dispute on a proposed amendment on abortion there will be pluralists on both sides but they will be reluctant to impose their view; they will have allowed the opposing view to enter into their thinking and — perhaps more importantly — their feelings.

Those who, like myself, are opposed to the amendment will have made the effort to appreciate the opposing arguments. They will have considered the possibility of the law against abortion being struck down by the Supreme Court; they will have thought about the argument that the foetus is a person with an absolute right to life and even if they disagree with it they will do so with some trepidation; they will have honestly faced the fact that if abortion is introduced it will be very difficult if not impossible to restrict it.

Those who favour the amendment will have genuinely considered the deep division in the community which the amendment will bring; they will have weighed up the value of the amendment against its sectarian appearance (and whatever about the reality the amendment has a sectarian appearance); they will have faced the fact that no matter how humane and caring our society is even remotely likely to become, the young unmarried mother, abandoned by the father of her child, is confronted by an appallingly difficult task; they will have recognized the enormous moral difference between the adult woman who failed to take sufficient precautions and the woman of any age but perhaps particularly the child violently raped.

To conclude and to repeat: pluralism is a general attitude which attempts the difficult task of attending to other views. From it nothing at all can be deduced. This may make it seem useless. Certainly the growth of pluralism in Ireland will not have quick results but in a society within which there *are* differing views, differing attitudes and differing aspirations pluralism seems a more hopeful route than a moral totalitarianism of whatever stamp.

The Constitution and the Right to Life

BERNARD TREACY, O.P.

Campaigners must speak in headlines if they are to present their case to a mass audience. Whether the campaign is pro-amendment or anti-amendment, there is a real danger that issues will become so simplified as to be distorted. This danger is particularly acute in constitutional debate. For the Irish Constitution is a subtle document which, because of the power of the Courts to interpret it, it has a vital quality. As it is read and applied by the judges, it provides protections and recognizes both rights and freedoms well beyond what a mere reading of the text would suggest.

This chapter is written from a purely legal point of view. The task is to state what the Constitution already teaches about the right to life, and what protection the law already gives to the unborn. There is also a consideration of the legal questions raised in the train of the campaign to insert a 'pro-life amendment' into the Constitution.

CONSTITUTION IS PRO-LIFE

The first point to be made is this: The Irish Constitution already recognizes and protects the right to life, as is clear from Article 40.3.2:

> The State shall, in particular, by its laws protect as best it may from unjust attack and in the case of injustice done, vindicate the life, person, good name, and property rights of every citizen.

No amendment is necessary to make the Irish Constitution 'pro-life'.

Does this guarantee of the right to life extend to the unborn? The answer is Yes. Twice Mr Justice Walsh in the Supreme Court has made such assertions. In an adoption case *(G. v. An Bord Uchatala),* he declared:

> [A child] has the right to life itself and the right to be guarded against all threats to its existence either before or after birth . . . The right to life necessarily involves the right to be born, the

right to preserve and defend, and to have preserved and defended, that life . . .[1]

Some years earlier in *Magee's* case (in which the Supreme Court recognized the right to marital privacy), the same Judge declared:

> Any action on the part of either the husband and wife or of the State to limit family sizes by endangering or destroying human life must necessarily not only be an offence against the common good but also against the guaranteed personal rights of the life in question.[2]

It is true that these comments are *obiter dicta,* statements made by a judge which were not strictly necessary in deciding the matter before the Court, and thus they are not technically binding. But they do have a very high persuasive value, and should not be lightly disregarded. *Obiter dicta* of one generation can become the settled law of later days.

A good example is the history of Irish judicial thinking on the question of recognizing foreign divorces, given the public policy contained in Article 41.3.3 of the Constitution. In *Mayo-Perrott's* case (1958) the point at issue was whether an award of costs in a foreign divorce could be enforced by the Irish courts. But the Supreme Court went on to consider the recognition of foreign divorce decrees, a matter which was clearly *obiter*. Although Chief Justice Maguire considered that the Constitution prohibited even the recognition of foreign divorces. Mr Justice Kingsmill Moore did not share this view. And when in 1971 the precise question of recognizing foreign divorces came to be decided in the High Court, Mr Justice Kenny chose in *Bank of Ireland v. Caffin* to adopt the views of Kingsmill Moore J. rather than those expressed by the Chief Justice. In 1975 the Supreme Court affirmed the correctness of Kenny J's approach, by deciding in *G. v. G.* not to recognize an English divorce which had been obtained without domicile, a decision which implies that there are circumstances in which foreign divorces can properly be recognized in the Irish Courts.

I have indulged in this digression on divorce law simply to show that *obiter dicta* in the Supreme Court cannot be dismissed as being without authority. Such comments from the bench are a clear

1. 113 ILTR 25.
2. 1974 IR 284.

indication of judicial thinking, signalling the direction in which the law can be expected to develop.

From this point of view it does seem likely that the Irish courts will continue to protect and defend the right to life as extending to the unborn.

JUDGES ARE NOT "UNDEMOCRATIC"

It is sometimes argued that the Irish Courts are likely to extend the right of marital privacy to include a right to abortion, and that such a decision would be undemocratic. There are two parts in this argument, and I wish to consider the second part first.

At various times since the 1960's the Supreme Court has been criticized from various quarters, being accused of acting in an undemocratic way when it recognizes and upholds the personal rights of the citizen. These allegations show a misunderstanding of the functions and duties of judges.

The Constitution itself explicitly gives to the High Court 'full original jurisdiction in and power to determine all matters and questions, whether of law or of fact'.[3] And the next sub-section of Article 34 goes on to state that 'the jurisdiction of the High Court shall extend to the validity of any law having regard to the provisions of this Constitution'. On appeal, the Supreme Court has a like jurisdiction; indeed the Constitution forbids the enacting of a law which would remove from the appellate jurisdiction of the Supreme Court the power to test the constitutionality of any law. Thus, when recognizing and enforcing constitutionally protected rights, the judges are doing no more than their duty, fulfilling a responsibility explicitly laid on them by the Constitution. There could be nothing undemocratic about that.

The Irish people have been well served by their judges both in the High Court and in the Supreme Court. And it is good to acknowledge the valuable contribution made by judges in defending the rights and liberties of the citizen.

WHAT RIGHTS ARE PROTECTED?

When interpreting the Constitution, as is their duty, the judges have recognized three categories of personal rights as being constitutionally protected. These categories are: rights explicitly set

3. Article 34.3.1.

out in the text of the Constitution; rights which are implicit in those set out in the text; and thirdly the Courts have recognized a reservoir of unspecified rights which cannot be related to the text of the Constitution, but which, because of the wording of Article 40.3.1, receive constitutional protection.

This third category has given rise to much controversy, and it may need some explanation. In 1963 Mr Justice Kenny in the High Court gave judgement in *Ryan v. Attorney General.* Mrs Gladys Ryan sought to have the Health (Flouridation of Water Supplies) Act declared unconstitutional as infringing, among other rights, her right to bodily integrity. This right is not listed in the text of the Constitution, nor can it be implied in any right actually listed. But it was argued that the right to bodily integrity was among those latent in the general expression 'personal rights'. Mr Justice Kenny held against the plaintiff on the facts, but he accepted that

> the personal rights which may be invoked to invalidate legislation are not confined to those specified in Article 40 but include all those rights which flow from the Christian and democratic nature of the State.[4]

With this doctrine the Supreme Court agreed.

This development is perfectly valid, for the text of Article 40.3 makes it clear that the personal rights mentioned in section 3.1

> are not exhausted by the enumeration of 'life, person, good name, and property rights' in section 3.2 as is shown by the use of the words 'in particular'; nor by the more detached treatment of specific rights in the subsequent sections of the article.[5]

Since *Ryan's* case and the recognition of the right to bodily integrity, there has been a growing list of rights which the courts recognize as enjoying constitutional protection. Some examples can be given: the right to have access to the courts *(Macauley v. Minister for Posts and Telegraphs);* the right to earn a livelihood *(Murtagh Properties v. Clery);* the right to travel *(The State (K.M.) v. Minister for Foreign Affairs);* the right of marital privacy *(Magee v. Attorney General and others).*

When the Supreme Court in 1974 recognized the right of marital

4. 1965 IR 294.
5. *Ibid.*

privacy, alarm bells began to ring in many quarters. The American
Supreme Court had moved in a few years from recognizing the right
of marital privacy to recognizing the right to abortion. And, the
argument ran, it is inevitable that the Irish Supreme Court will go the
same way.[6]

DOES MARITAL PRIVACY IMPLY ABORTION?

Can the Irish Supreme court be expected to follow the American
example by expanding the right of marital privacy in such a way as to
allow for abortion? It is true that the concept of marital privacy has
proved to be a pliable one in American jurisprudence, and that, when
articulating that concept, the Irish judges made extensive use of
American decisions. But it does not follow that an Irish court will
develop the concept as it has been developed across the Atlantic.

For one thing, the reasoning in *Wade's* case (the American
precedent allowing for abortion) is generally considered to be very
poor; and it has been so severely criticized in legal journals that, it is
submitted, another court would not now adopt the arguments
accepted in *Wade*.

Irish public policy already recognizes that the unborn child is in
some sense a legal person. An example can be drawn from the Civil
Liabilities Act. Section 58 lays down that

> the law relating to wrongs shall apply to an unborn child for his
> protection in like manner as if the child were born, provided the
> child is subsequently born alive.

This means that if a child in the womb suffers damage, the child
herself, once born, can sue the wrongdoer who caused the damage,
and can recover compensation. Under such an arrangement the child
in the womb is not regarded as merely a piece of plasma. The unborn
child is clearly regarded as being the subject of rights. For if the child,
even in the womb, is not the subject of rights, it suffered no loss of
rights, no *injury,* at the time it suffered damage; and therefore would
have no right to sue. The child in the womb is in this sense the subject
of rights, and thus is in some measure recognized in Irish law as being
a person.

6. For a full and detailed discussion of this controversy, see James O'Reilly,
'Marital Privacy and Family Law', *Studies* Spring 1977, p. 8; and William Binchy,
'Marital Privacy and Family Law: A Reply to Mr O'Reilly', *Studies* Winter 1977, p.
330.

Here is another reason for suggesting that the Irish courts are unlikely to follow the American example by expanding the right of marital privacy by allowing for abortion.

Furthermore, the right of marital privacy as described by the Supreme Court in *Magee's* case, is a very precise matter indeed. It is not as elastic as commentators have suggested. Two judges (Walsh and Griffin JJ.) explicitly ruled out an extension of the right to allow abortion. The right is enjoyed by married people, and not by the general public. (There is no discrimination here, for Article 40.1 recognizes that the State may have due regard in its enactments to differences of capacity and social function). The right of marital privacy means simply that the State may not prevent married couples from importing contraceptives for private use. The ban on the sale of contraceptives and on their importation for sale remained unaffected by the Court's decision in 1974. (A post-*Magee* statute, the Health (Family Planning) Act, 1978, now allows the sale of contraceptives in limited circumstances).

Because the American decisions allowing abortion have been so cogently criticized in legal literature, because Irish public policy already regards the unborn child as the subject of rights, and because the right of marital privacy, as enunciated by the Supreme Court, is so very precise and carefully circumscribed, it is suggested that an Irish Supreme Court is very unlikely to follow the American example. There are no substantial grounds to fear that the Irish Supreme Court will expand the right of marital privacy to allow a right to abortion.

A STATUTE IS NEEDED

The rights of the unborn child are further protected by Section 58 of the Offences Against the Person Act, 1861, which declares:

> Every woman being with child who, with intent to procure her own miscarriage, shall unlawfully administer to herself any poison or other noxious thing, or shall unlawfully use any instrument or other means whatsoever with the like intent, and whosoever, with intent to procure the miscarriage of any woman, whether she be or be not with child, shall unlawfully administer to her or cause to be taken by her any poison or other noxious thing, or shall unlawfully use any instrument or other means whatsoever with the like intent, shall be guilty of an offence, and being convicted thereof, shall be liable . . . to imprisonment for life . . .

The general meaning is clear: It is a crime to carry out an abortion, at whatever stage in the pregnancy; and both the mother and the person who conducts the operation will be guilty. But there seem to be exceptions, as indicated by the use of adverb 'unlawfully'. This suggests that there may be situations in which 'administering a poison . . . or using an instrument' to bring about a miscarriage would not be unlawful. What are those exceptions?

No clear answer can be given because there have been no decisions in the Irish courts on this point. But a 1939 English case, *R. v. Bourne,* which concerned a charge under Section 58 of the 1861 Act, may offer some guidance.

Dr Bourne had carried out an abortion at the request of the parents of a thirteen-year-old girl who had conceived as a result of multiple rape by a group of soldiers. The trial judge, Mr Justice MacNaghten, was guided by the Infant Life Preservation Act, 1929, which provided that a person shall not be guilty of the offence of child destruction if it be proved that the act which caused the death of the child was done in good faith for the purpose only of preserving the life of the mother. Now, this defence is not available in Ireland, for the Infant Life Preservation Act 1929 is a British Act; and the judge went beyond the words of the Act in holding that the preservation of life included the preservation of health. However, the judge did state that the words 'for the purpose only of preserving the life of the mother' represented the common law, and thus were implicit in the 1861 Act by virtue of the word 'unlawfully'.

If these words do represent the pre-1861 common law, it could be argued that they thereby declare the position in Irish law. If so, an Irish court could validly adopt the view that procuring a miscarriage would not be 'unlawful' in regard to Section 58 of The Offences Against The Person Act if it were procured in good faith for the purpose only of preserving the life of the mother. However, the doctrine in unclear; and clarification would be welcome. This could come either from an Act of the Oireachtas of by decisions in the courts. But court cases occur in such a haphazard way that doctrines are handed down piecemeal. It would be altogether better to have a clear statement both of the principle of protecting the life of the foetus and of the exceptions, if any, which may be needed; and this would be best provided in a statute.

DRAFTING DIFFICULTIES

It would seem that the fears expressed by the 'Pro-Life Amendment

Campaign' are not grounded in actual defects in Irish law or in the Constitution which, as interpreted to date, already affords a real measure of protection to the unborn child. Rather their fears arise from apprehension about what the courts may do in some hypothetical future situation, against which they want to 'copperfasten' the rights of the unborn.

This project seems to be surrounded by many practical difficulties, as is borne out by the reports that successive Attorneys General have had great difficulty in trying to draft an amendment to meet the campaigners' aims.

Either the amendment has to exclude all interventions which could jeopardise the life of the foetus, or it has to allow for exceptions. The first alternative is one nobody wants. And the second gives rise to real difficulties. For if exceptions are to be allowed, we must all trust the judges in their interpretation of these exceptions. But the pro-amendment campaign seems to be unwilling to trust the judiciary.

Furthermore, serious problems arise when considering how the exceptions could be drafted. Presumably the pro-amendment campaign would not want a formula which, for instance, would outlaw such necessary procedures as operations for cancer during pregnancy. Most moral thinkers accept that an operation to remove a cancerous uterus, even if it contains a foetus, is a valid moral choice. But if this choice is justified by reference to the 'principle of the act of double effect', it becomes extremely difficult to reconcile with legal philosophy.

The principle of the act of double effect presumes that it is possible to separate the good effect intended (e.g. saving the woman's life by curing the cancer) from the secondary evil effect which is not intended but only permitted (e.g. the death of the foetus). But civil law views human activity in quite a different way. Legally a person is presumed to intend the foreseeable consequences of his actions. Thus, if a man deliberately sells a gun to another for use in murdering a third, he may be interested only in the cash profit to be made out of the sale, but he will be held by a court to intend to aid the murderer.[7] In the same way, in the amputaiton of a cancerous uterus, a doctor would be held by a court to intend the death of the foetus because that is a foreseeable consequence of the operation. The doctor would be saved from legal guilt only by an explicit declaration, either in an act of parliament or from a judge, that in this case procuring the death of the foetus was not unlawful.

7. Devlin J. in *National Coal Board v. Gamble* 1958, 3 All E R 203.

Thus to discuss a constitutional amendment 'copperfastening' the rights of the unborn in terms drawn from traditional moral theology presents a very serious legal difficulty. It involves a clash of cultures, a confrontation between ways of viewing the world. Moral theology would say that removing the cancerous uterus is not abortion because the death of the foetus is not directly willed. The law would say that the operation is abortion because the death of the foetus can be foreseen. It is not easy to see how the world-view of the theologians can successfully be translated into terms acceptable to the common law.

The Pro-Amendment Campaign wants to 'copperfasten' the right to life of the unborn. It is, however, unclear whether this can be achieved in a Constitution which recognizes that there is no such thing as an absolute and unqualified fundamental right. Even where family rights are described as 'inalienable and imprescriptible', Article 42 itself allows that there may be circumstances in which the State is obliged to take the place of parents. Most other rights are expressly qualified in the text of the Constitution. The right to freedom of conscience and of religious practice, to take one example, can be exercised by the citizens 'subject to public order and morality'.[8]

In this context it would be anomalous to grant to one group of persons within the State, e.g. the unborn, a copperfastened right which would in every circumstance override the rights of another group, e.g. mothers. Equally, it would be anomalous to grant to mothers a right which would override the rights and claims of the unborn. What is needed is a clear recognition that the unborn do enjoy the right to life, within machinery for resolving the problems where conflicts of rights arise. This is best done by recognizing that real conflicts of rights can arise, and by leaving the resolution of those conflicts to the courts, as at present.

RIGHTS CONFINED TO CITIZENS?

I have argued that the Irish Constitution already protects the right to life, and that this protection extends to the unborn. I have shown that the unborn are further protected from unjust attack by Section 58 of the Offences Against The Person Act, 1861. I have suggested that it is very unlikely that an Irish court would, even in a heart-rending case, declare the 1861 Act to be repugnant to a constitutionally

8. Article 44.2.1.

protected right to privacy such as would allow for abortion. Does it follow that the right to life is perfectly protected by the Irish Constitution?

The frank answer is No. There is a real difficulty, broader than the questions raised by the pro-life amendment campaigners. The difficulty is this: The text of the Constitution speaks of the right to life and other personal rights being enjoyed by 'citizens'. This seems to imply that for non-citizens their personal rights are not constitutionally protected. It seems that a visitor, or long-stay resident from France, or Britain, or Nigeria, or wherever, is not protected in his personal fundamental rights as a citizen would be.

The question is a very difficult one which came before the courts in *The State (Nicolau) v. An Bord Uchtala.* Mr Nicolau, a British subject, sought an order of the High Court to prevent his (illegitimate) child being adopted, and challenged the constitutionality of the Adoption Act 1952, as infringing his constitutionally protected personal right as a natural father. The Attorney General refrained from arguing that Mr Nicolau, a non-citizen, had lesser rights under the Constitution than a citizen has. But Mr Justice Henchy said:

> I hold that neither Article 40.1 nor 40.3 confers on the prosecutor any constitutional rights.[9]

It will be remembered that Article 40.3 enunciates the Constitution's protection of the right to life.

The Supreme Court, however, was clearly embarrassed by the matter, and it

> expressly reserved for another and more appropriate case consideration of the effect of non-citizenship upon the interpretation of [Articles 40, 41, 42.9].[10]

Thus, the matter has not been decided against the non-citizen.

At present the courts certainly would give constitutional protection to the personal rights of all those living in the State, regardless of whether they are citizens. For natural law thinking now holds sway in the Irish courts. Judges insist that fundamental rights are not *granted* by law, not even by the Constitution. Rather, they inhere in every human being, by virtue of being human, and they are

9. 1966 IR 567.
10. *Ibid.*

recognized and protected by the law. A short quotation from Mr Justice Walsh shows the pattern of judicial thinking:

> In this country it falls finally upon the judges to interpret the Constitution and in doing so to determine where necessary the rights which are superior and antecedent to positive law . . . In particular the terms of Article 40.3 expressly subordinate the law to justice . . . natural rights, or human rights, are not created by law but . . .the Constitution confirms their existence and gives them protection.[11]

As long as such thinking prevails, non-citizens will suffer no diminution of personal rights in Ireland. But the text of Article 40 remains a worry. All classes and groups would be better protected if the text of the Constitution guaranteed to protect the fundamental rights, not just of citizens, but of all persons living in the State.

11. *Magee v. Attorney General* 1974 IR 318.

Defence of the Silent and Unseen

JANE LINDEN

WHEN DOES HUMAN LIFE BEGIN?

A human life begins at conception when a living cell from the father fertilises a living cell from the mother. From that moment the mother's body sustains the new life which is developing.

Seven days after the egg has been fertilised the tiny embryo attaches itself to the lining of the womb. Eight weeks later the inch-long foetus is recognisably human. At sixteen weeks the mother can feel the baby moving. At twenty four weeks the child has a chance of surviving after birth. And from this time onwards the unborn baby makes breathing movements, sucks its thumb, and even sleeps in the womb. Forty weeks after conception the baby is born, and starts on a new phase of its growth.

Modern scientific knowledge of life before birth has enabled us to see conception, growth in the womb, birth, infancy and even childhood as stages in development. In this development there is the gradual fulfilment of potential, potential which is present even in the tiniest embryo.

Christians used to ask themselves: At what moment did the unborn child receive a soul? They wanted to decide when a foetus became fully human because killing a baby, before or after birth, was a more grave sin than killing a foetus which had no soul.

Biological knowledge has led Catholics of today to realise that there is no moment when we can say 'that foetus is now a baby and must not be harmed'. We see that life develops continuously. We believe that no one has the right to interfere in that process and bring innocent life to an end.

HUMAN RIGHTS

Catholics are not the only people who insist on the rights of the unborn and reject abortion. A person who views all actions simply in terms of human rights will also defend the unborn, seeing as good those actions which enhance and preserve rights, while those which attack or undermine rights are held to be wrong.

The first of all rights is the right to life.

RIGHTS OF THE UNBORN

Do the unborn have rights? Not only Catholics answer Yes. So do most legal systems, even those that allow abortions.

In Britain, for instance, the law protects the right of the unborn to be free from harm. Thus, children injured in the womb when their mothers were prescribed the drug thalidomide, were entitled to compensation. Even when in the womb they enjoyed legally protected rights.

The 1967 British Abortion Act, under whose terms 140,000 abortions a year are performed, attempts to permit abortion in certain circumstances without detracting from the fundamental principle of law, the protection of life. For this reason the Act is framed in a negative way: Termination of pregnancy will not be considered a crime provided conditions laid down by the law are met. The upper time limit for abortion is twenty eight weeks. After that the child's life in the womb is inviolable.

Where is the logic in that? How did the child acquire an absolute right to life at twenty eight weeks when at twenty seven weeks, in certain cases, it did not have that right? Perhaps it is that the human right to life is granted by the state, which may, therefore, fix the moment at which rights begin and end. There are few people who would agree to that proposition.

When we look at abortion from the point of view of the unborn and their rights, we cannot make sense of it.

RIGHTS OF WOMAN

Some women argue that the complete dependance of the foetus on the mother's body means that its rights, if any, are subordinate to hers. She has the right to choose whether she will carry the child to term. According to this kind of argument, the foetus attains true personal rights at about twenty eight weeks, when it is capable of independent physical existence.

Medical science is constantly pushing back the time limit of what is called viability. That's why some of those who favour a woman's right to choose would like to see abortion forbidden after the twenty fourth week.

Viability, the capacity to live an independent physical life, cannot be a test of foetal rights. Equally, it is not acceptable to hold that because the child in the womb cannot survive without its mother, it must be regarded as an extension of its mother, an extension over which she has the power of life and death.

Biologically, an embryo, however immature, is quite distinct from its mother. Half its genetic make-up comes from the father and not from her. The separate life of the child must be respected.

Real difficulties arise if the mother's own health is in danger. Cases where the only way to save a mother's life is directly and intentionally to terminate the child's life are exceedingly rare. So, it is unrealistic and misleading to discuss abortion in terms of such extreme and unusual cases. But one comment can be made: Both mother and child have rights, and both sets of rights must be defended.

What, then, are the mother's rights if she does not have the right to end the pregnancy?

She has the right to all the moral and material support necessary for her own well-being and that of her child; the two cannot be separated. A society that does not recognise these rights but at the same time forbids abortion places impossible burdens on women.

The right to support is a right which truly protects a woman because it relieves her of pressure to get rid of her child. This pressure often comes from its father or her own parents who do not want the shame or burden of helping.

So, defending the child is also the defence of the mother to be what she is and most often wants to be, the supporter and guardian of life in her womb.

ABORTION FOR THE DEFORMED

Deformed children are a special responsibility for their parents and for society. Each year in Britain 15,000 children are born with serious defects, about 1-2% of live births. In Ireland in 1979 there were eleven handicapped children among each thousand live births.

Some of these babies have inherited their disorder, for instance those born with cystic fibrosis, a defect of the lungs. Others have been affected by contact with diseases like German measles. And recently there have been well-publicised cases of babies damaged by drugs like thalidomide.

In a minority of cases, where the mother is known to be likely to bear a handicapped child, accurate diagnosis before birth is possible. For instance, at sixteen weeks a little of the fluid that surrounds the baby in the womb may be drawn off and examined. Downe's Syndrome may be detected by this procedure.

A mother given this type of information may be thrown into mental agony: What should she do?

Catholics believe she should do nothing. Handicapped babies have the same rights as healthy ones. No physical or mental defect can take away the right of an adult to life. How can the case of a child be different?

The rights of the handicapped are just as strong as the rights of the healthy. But society must act to make those rights effective. Without support for them and their families, talk of the rights of the handicapped is empty.

A CHRISTIAN VIEW IN CHRISTIAN LANGUAGE

So far, we have discussed the problem of abortion in purely humanist terms. Even in those terms abortion cannot be justified.

Christians, however, do not see people only as bundles of rights but as children of God. All must be treated equally as children of God. Christians have always felt a special responsibility towards the weak, the sick, the poor, the victims of injustice, and towards sinners.

The Christian defence of the unborn is the defence of the silent and the unseen, who have only the Church to speak on their behalf. The Church believes that God loves unborn children, and asks us to love and protect them.

Catholics are not just *against abortion;* they are *for life.*

They defend the child in the womb for the same reasons they condemn weapons of mass destruction, murder, torture, summary execution, and the starvation of the poor by the rich.

The Church wants to see a world in which peace and justice reign, for it believes that this is a world created by God for all humankind, including unborn children.

Sanity and Abortion

ANNE SMITH

PART ONE

Sanity is a word which springs to our lips. We all imagine we know what we mean by the word. But the notion, of what it really is, changes subtly from generation to generation and from culture to culture. Although we are not all sure to agree on what exactly sanity is, we will probably all agree that it is a very desirable frame of mind to possess or to adopt!

Sanity would appear to have something to do with the delicate balance of the human mind. When this enviable equilibrium is disturbed one may be seen to act in ways considered, by the people around one, to be abnormal or in, modern parlance, one is considered mentally-ill. Of course it stands to reason that one runs the risk, when one is in the company of the mad, of being pronounced mad by them because one is sane.

Sanity is like a tight rope along which each of us must travel — across the valleys of our minds — down all our days until we reach eternity.

MUDDLING THROUGH TO ETERNITY

We teeter precariously, swaying first one way and then the other, amid the 'slings and arrows of outrageous fortune'. Survival and happiness (which man thinks, in his sane innocence, to be synonymous) are the carrots held out to lure us on as we set out across life's tightrope. Of course we never succeed in reaching those carrots because they are not real. Survival and happiness are myths or ideals (depending on whether you are an optimist or a pessimist) and unattainable this side of Heaven. We will in the long run neither survive death nor be happy for any length of time!

What, in fact, will happen has been happening to the teeming millions who have gone before us. Most of them and most of us (the great unwashed as we used to be called) muddle through our existence, feeling rather than thinking our way, until we die, inevitably, of natural causes or otherwise. This muddling through is conspicuously free of dialectic aid of any kind but is done, for the most part, with the help of a home-spun philosophy composed of common sense and the grace of God.

Of course the highly educated among us, dazed by their own learning, see this simple truth only in flashes of blessed intuition (and that only the wisest of them)! It is all too simple, by far, for their devious complex minds to accept. Its very simplicity bores them! These magnates of the mind prefer to set great store by their reason and they imagine they can better our world by the use of it. We pride ourselves (clever folk and simple folk alike) on being civilised. Our politicians, scientists, philosophers and churchmen strike attitudes of grave pomposity. They impress us as they strut about and deliberate and calculate and assure us that we, the Human Race, are all important to the Creator's Plan. They insist on the importance of man being seen to be at the helm of the ship of Human Destiny guiding it into a quiet harbour in Utopia. God has watched it all, heretofore, with great imperturbability but no doubt we will surprise him into raising his divine eyebrow if and when we succeed in blowing up the planet!

FACING REALITY

Without being at all sure what reality really is, we talk at length about it and we urge one another to face it! Most of the poor unfortunates I know who have been forced, by adverse fortune, to face reality are in fact dead (some by their own hand) or else they wish they were dead. Many of these have been pronounced mentally ill by their peers and their betters who presume themselves to be normal. Of course most ordinary common or garden folk are too busy muddling through to pay much attention to reality or to the daft. They tend to ignore them. If the mentally ill get troublesome then they lock them up (that is after they get the clever ones to pronounce them mad!)

To my mind there is only one way whereby reality can be looked at and endured with any degree of sanity and that is by virtue of hope — the wild, mad hope that there is such a force as love operating in all creation. Without the warmth of being in love coursing through one, one's existence is a curse. One can love anything and everything which strikes one as beautiful. A man can love a woman or vice versa or he can love a child or mankind *en masse*. He can love a cause or ideas and of course some noble souls love love itself — these are the truly alive and they believe in a benevolent God in spite of any apparent evidence to the contrary. These noble souls are not very logical but I have to admit they are sane!

MENTALLY ILL

I want to be sane also but I can only feel sane now and then in waves of joy. Alas very often I fall away into insanity when I doubt the goodness of God. Then I become mentally-ill. To be mentally-ill is to be very very human and vulnerable. If I were a simple animal or had no education at all or were mentally handicapped none of this trauma would be taking place in my mind. If I were simply a cow I would not know any of the things I have had to work out for myself by the sweat of my cerebral brow. I would instead sense reality in every bone in my body and in all its splendid simplicity. I'd gaze at a distant hedge, and chew my cud, contentedly, accepting reality. This, of course, would last only for a short time because very soon a member of the human species would be sure to come along and eat me!

Who can deny that life depends on killing — the very balance of nature depends on it — we must accept that reality, but do we have to kill so wantonly, caring so little about the methods we use to rob another living creature, man or animal, of its precious existence? Do we ever think of whether our fly killing sprays (which are used so liberally) are causing deaths by agony when, with our brains we could easily find a way of reducing the number of flies by some less painful method. It is so easy to scoff and to say that flies don't matter: but I believe we will never better our world until we better it for all living things, for animals and plants as well as for ourselves. Our Bishops tell us that human life is sacred. Of course it is, but why do they not tell us that all life is precious and sacred and potentially beautiful? Why don't they tell us to treat all living things with tenderness (even our killing should be done with love). Until we learn to care about flies we are not going to care about the defenceless human foetus whose existence and power to feel pain we can only guess at?

PART TWO

Since the first rocket was blasted off to the moon from planet earth even plain people, people like myself (who are not scientists or physicists) have come to be aware of certain laws of which we were ignorant hitherto. Now we know that no strong force exists without the aid of the energy it derives from its equally strong and powerful backlash. It has been borne in on us, as we reflect on these things, that we cannot really be said to know or understand any phenomenon unless we study its opposite. We would not recognise inclement weather unless we had known fine days with sun and balmy breezes. We would have no concept of peace or equanimity unless we experienced turmoil and war. Without death we could not understand life; without sorrow joy to us would seen insipid. Some of us have doubts about our own existence (but only very clever folk), most of the rest of us are absolutely certain we exist (especially when we are in pain). Some clever folk worry themselves sick about the possible existence of non-existence. Mankind is the only species capable of rebelling against its own existence and it does so when it entertains the death-wish, either compulsively or voluntarily.

DON'T IGNORE THE DEATH-WISH

The will to live or exist is one of the strongest urges mankind experiences; but the will to live is counter-balanced by the death-wish which manifests itself as anger and aggression. If we want goodwill (or the will to live) to predominate in the lives of peoples, we must have great respect for the anger and aggression of the oppressed among us. We ignore the anger, in those who wish to die, at our peril. This anger cannot be stamped out or suppressed or it will break out inevitably in ever more violent ways in murders, suicides, war and civil unrest. It would be wise of society as a whole to study the anger of the mentally-ill (as these disturbed people are so often called). We should try, as much as lies in our power, to understand and assuage their anger. The death-wish is felt in the conscious mind of the mentally ill but it is there in all of us, hidden in the recesses of our subconscious ready to surface should we ever be subjected to intolerable pressures and come to experience our existence as unendurable. The will to live flickers, however tentatively, in even the most suicidal among us, nevertheless, it is impossible to remove this troublesome death-wish without simultaneously removing the will to live. Society, as a whole, experiences this battle between the opposing wills — to live or to die. In different ages we see first one of these gain ascendancy and then the other in another age.

In those ages when the will to die predominates in the consciousness of society there is an increase of suicides and abortions and other manifestation of disenchantment with life. During these violent eras there is a tendency to see God as malevolent (the temptation then of course is not to believe in him at all — a malevolent

God is too frightening a concept to be entertained for long). At the present time it would seem that society is in the grip of a collective will to die.

A SUICIDAL AGE

The main moral issue in today's world is — do we or do we not succumb to the death-wish? There is a great temptation to throw in the sponge and allow everything to end in what we are slowly coming to believe is inevitable — a nuclear holocaust. Events seem to have a momentum all their own — apart from whatever we may intend should or should not happen — we are on a slippery ski slope. Many of our young people have given up trying to live by opting out into mere existence, seeking oblivion in loud music drugs, sex and non involvement with the establishment. Most of all they wish they had never been born. The basic feeling in our age is suicidal.

Nevertheless the will to live is still trying to work its way up to the forefront of our consciousness. We have hidden fears of genocide. Because of this fear and because of the fascination of the death-wish, of which I am very much aware myself, I am afraid I cannot support legalised death-dealing of any kind — war, capital punishment, euthanasia or abortion. I know these violent things will happen, they are part of the warp and woof of the fabric of human existence. Only God knows why it happens and he will be our judge. He, and only he, knows why violence is at the very centre of life — without it there would be no life! Life and death are the opposite sides of the same reality; only those who have endured the full torture and the ecstasy of life can be said to have really faced reality.

Although I'm unable (while I'm sane that is) to support any form of violence at the same time I am equally unable to support any legalised form of punishment (or counter violence) against those who in their pain resort to any of the above methods of seeking death to end unendurable pain. Even capital punishment will be resorted to, justifiably, at times of great social unrest, when society as a whole, in pain and in fear for its survival, feels it needs to protect itself from anarchy. Passive resistance is the only violence that should be resorted to by the objective; violence in cold blood and after *objective* deliberation is always evil, I think.

When we address ourselves to the problem of a woman who genuinely 'feels' desperately that she *must* have an abortion we are presented with a problem to which, at present anyway, we will not find a logical answer. If we pride ourselves on being a caring society

(and we try to) then we must identify with the pain of the woman and
with the pain and the danger to the tiny foetus in her womb. The
woman is in danger also — the danger lies in her own will to die which
will surface under the terrible pressures she must be feeling, from
within and without, to have brought her to the point where she wants
to do violence to herself and to her extended self — which is her
offspring!

In my opinion (and I've been pregnant seven times and very
unhappily so for some of these pregnancies) no *normal* woman would
consider abortion while it is morally and socially taboo unless she
were under intolerable pressure and felt that her existence was
unendurable (which would render her abnormal). The problem we are
faced with today is the fact that for some odd reason the idea of
enduring an unwanted pregnancy is now more taboo than the idea of
killing the foetus. The reasoning behind this new taboo is that it is
thought that an unwanted baby must in time become an unhappy
unwanted person. My only answer to that is to say that I was a very
'wanted' baby (I was my parents' first child) and I grew up to wish I
had never been born! Especially so did I feel this at the time I suffered
a nervous breakdown on the birth of my mentally handicapped son.
No child in my womb was ever in danger of death from abortion but
my mentally handicapped is in some danger of dying. Sometimes
when I am terribly depressed and I cannot cope with life I begin to
think that I could solve all our family's problems (and they are many
and often painful) by giving my son (who is handicapped and yet is so
precious to me) an overdose of sleeping tablets and then to take them
myself; because I realise that when I am normal I would never be able
to live with the thought of what I had done. When I'm feeling
suicidal, God seems lost to me; I am utterly alone — I feel I do not
have to justify my actions to anyone. There is then, I feel, nobody I
care about and nobody who cares about me. How can someone like
me condemn a woman who resorts to abortion for some
overwhelming subjective reason of her own. Does it matter to me or
to a woman desperately in need of an abortion what the Irish
Constitution says or does not say? The Constitution is written by the
ordinary run of humankind — man and women who have never been
driven to the point of wishing to die; but what about the ones who
have? They are citizens and human also — they are humanity
exposed in all its agony!

I for one am going to abstain from voting in the forthcoming
Referendum. I believe we should not have this put before us at all. It
serves no purpose; it will in my opinion merely increase the pain

inherent in every abortion situation and in the long run be ineffective. A woman who is hell-bent on having an abortion will find a way willy-nilly or kill herself in the process! We should tread softly, since the issue at stake is the sanity of mankind as a whole! When I hear that we are about to produce legislation to ensure that a man or woman, who even once drives while drunk, will be barred from driving for life then I might come down off the fence and begin to believe that we are really getting down to tackle the mindless risks society still takes in regard to human life and its sacredness!

Pluralism: Justice or the Interests of the Stronger

FERGAL O'CONNOR, O.P.

In the debate about the referendum and in the broad and fairly general discussion about our constitution, the notion of pluralism plays a key role. A closer look at this concept may help to clarify some of the issues.

In its origins, pluralism was a philosophical attitude to the person, society and the state, and there were both secular and religious, individualist and socialist, Anglo-Saxon and continental versions of the idea. It was, in part, a reaction to state absolutism and the growing tendency to bureaucratized control of life. On the positive side, it stressed the freedom and rights of individuals and groups to live according to their own cultural, religious and social beliefs and practices, stressing the primacy of society over the state, the individual over both, and social power over state power. Within it were strong elements of both individualism and that form of socialism which sought to reduce the power and influence of the state in favour of its component groups.[1]

POLITICAL PLURALISM

This version of the idea has been described as political pluralism because there is concern with political structures and the relationship of the state to the smaller social groupings within it. Pluralists argue for maximum autonomy for the group; and while they recognize the need for state authority to create the wider *milieu* where such groups

1. The skeletal image of political pluralism outlined here refers mainly to the English version. Its roots lie in the Whig distrust of power and in the negative side of the liberal tradition expressed most forcefully by, for example, Lord Acton. A few names will suffice: J. N. Figgis, C. D. H. Cole, H. Laski and Bertrand Russell. Each of these men expounded some version of the idea, but they fleshed out the concept in different ways and each of them did so differently at different stages in his own development. The doctrine has many 'cousins', all of which give a relative primacy to the smaller group, however defined, and an ancillary or service role to the state, which is frequently described as 'a society of societies', or a 'community of communities'. It is impossible to reflect all shades of usage: the concept has been appropriated by such disparate theorists as federalists and fascists. Obviously, at a certain point the concept loses its identity.

could flourish, they want it to be severely circumscribed. They wish to assert that the rights of individuals and groups are antecedent to and independent of the state, and that any claim by the state to legal, political and moral sovereignty is without foundation. In effect, they want to conceive the social and political order as having been built from the ground upwards, with the state being defined as the least significant part. Above all, they see their theories as an attempt to describe an ideal social and political order.

Their views were, of course, derived from a deep and passionate concern for the freedom and dignity of the individual and the smaller group. They insisted that liberty was a fundamental political value, and that liberty is best served in a state where power is decentralized and shared by the many subordinate groupings whose origins and identity are manifold, for example religious, cultural, industrial, professional, etc. The notion of liberty implicit in their teaching was never clearly defined by them. For all of them the idea of freedom of conscience was central and some of these theorists, especially those from within the Church of England who sought the disestablishment of the Church, discussed the idea of the secular state but the notion was never clearly defined. It did of course mean that the state should not enforce any particular religion, but this wasn't the issue. From the pluralist point of view the aim was rather to stop the state meddling in the inner life of the smaller groups, secular or religious.[2]

We must not confuse this doctrine of pluralism with the many and various other forms of argument in favour of toleration and religious freedom. The concept of pluralism is a much wider concept and in a sense is intelligible only as a reaction to the fully developed modern concept of the state as a *locus* of power, authority and sovereignty quite separate from its citizens and from any other subordinate groupings.[3] It was then an attempt to stop the growth of this monster

2. J. N. Figgis, for example, was concerned with the effects which 'establishment' had on the Church of England and, on a wider scale, with the general ecclesiastical tendency towards centralization. Indeed, all pluralists were reacting against the prevailing belief that centralization and the growth of bureaucracy were not only inevitable but desirable in all organizations, large or small. The Roman Catholic teaching on *subsidiarity* was aimed at the secular versions of this process. Vatican II, however, raised the issue within the Church itself and the doctrine of collegiality was a step towards the recognition of some sort of pluralism within the Roman Catholic Church. The ideas that emerged on ecumenism hinted at a kind of pluralism within the wider fold of Christianity.

3. These claims had been given a new dignity by the development of nationalism, which in its more rhetorical forms gave the nation-state a kind of mystical being. In the struggle for political freedom, the maxim 'to every nation its own state' was often taken to mean 'every state must be one nation'. Self-appointed spokesmen for the

and to re-assert the service image of the state vis-à-vis the individual and the subordinate groups.

The concept is still operative particularly in England, and the schizophrenia of British socialism may derive in part from the fact that the notion played a large part in the development of the trade union consciousness. But this consciousness was later modified by a form of statism. Pluralism and statism however cannot blend together. The British Labour Party is based on the idea of the autonomy of the trade union movement (it should be free to order its own affairs); and on the idea that it is entitled to use its group power to control the power of the state, to shape and mould the life of the nation according to its own vision of things. Tony Benn's brand of socialism and democracy are a very good example of this impossible marriage of pluralism and statism.[4]

In general, political pluralism was advocated as a moral, social and political principle. As a psychological attitude it implied a sort of rugged determination on the part of individuals and groups to be self-caring and self-creating.[5]

MORAL PLURALISM

There is, however, another and, perhaps more radical, version of the

---

nation could make unlimited demands on individuals and on subordinate groups to behave in certain ways as a condition of membership. Many of the post-colonial countries have created great problems for themselves by seeking to impose an unreal unity as a supporting base for their new state.

4. The theory of 'workers' control' espoused by some of the British Left is an attempt to restore authority to the local, or subordinate group. However, it is, in some of its forms, tinged with a great deal of statism and, in others, with anarchism. Either way, it differs from political pluralism.

5. There is another and very modern sense of political pluralism propounded by political scientists and sociologists, either as an ideal or as a *de facto* political process. It exists wherever we have a number of interest groups each seeking to use the power of the state for its own purposes. In this view, the role of the state is to conciliate these differing interest groups, not on the basis of some objective sense of justice, but rather on the basis of a common interest with which all can identify. A special case is the theory of power elites according to which power is shared or competed for by a number of defined elites in a particular state. This version of pluralism is synonymous with pressure-group politics and is widely accepted as the only viable form of advanced democracy. It is of course the reverse of the notion of political pluralism outlined here, though it is often confused with it. As I indicate in the article, what passes as political pluralism is very often pressure-group politics in action. I have not discussed this version of pluralism since many people would regard it, at least in theory, as a corruption of the pluralist ideal. Nor have I discussed a number of related sociological theories which use the terms 'plural', or 'pluralist' but in different senses.

principle based on the fact that all our ideals cannot be simultaneously realized. There is, the argument goes, an inevitable and irreconcilable conflict of values and ideals because men create different absolutes for themselves and rational reconciliation of these is impossible. Thus order and liberty, authority and justice, security and happiness may all conflict with each other and each of us will give primacy to one or the other. Hence the desire to solve the evils of the world within some sort of coherent single vision is a Utopian dream doomed to fail. History teaches us that this yearning for a final systematic solution of this conflict of ideals brings nothing but suffering and misery on mankind.

In this version of pluralism the individual and his right to chose is given a relative primacy limited in each historical context by the commonly held views as to what is wicked or shameful or evil. Thus decisions will be made at different times in favour of certain values and these decisions will entail the curtailing of the liberty of some individuals and perhaps the coercing of others. They will not be made on the basis of some universal, single principle whether it comes from a secular or religious vision, but on the practical moral demands of the situation. The individual, according to this view, must not be sacrificed to any transcendent goal, present or future. This version of pluralism has deep roots in the past but its modern forms in the Anglo-Saxon countries tend to find their roots in Mill although the *rationale* is different.

Pluralism, so defined, is based on two truths about human nature. First, that there is a virtual infinity of ideals, each noble in its own way but all are not simultaneously realizable; hence the description, moral pluralism. Second, that there is no certitude as to how they might be reconciled in general or indeed in many particular situations; hence the need to safeguard the inner moral character of the individual person from unnecessary and unjustifiable coercion by individuals or groups.[6]

6. I have called this version 'moral pluralism' because it is generally stated in terms of a pluralism of values, of moral views or visions of life and attacks the temptation to absolutise any one set of values or any one vision to which all others should be subordinated. Similarly, we can talk about philosophical and theological pluralism, suggesting the inevitable limitation of any theoretical system. I take Isaiah Berlin as the most eloquent contemporary exponent of this view and he himself traces it to Mill, Constant, Tocqueville and, indirectly and ingeniously, to Machiavelli. Berlin would reject any suggestion that his views lead to a crude moral relativism which argues that all moral positions are equally true. It is because he believes that the right course of action must be found by the person in his or her unique historical situation that he rejects all *a priori*, monist and determinist solutions to moral-political

Because of these beliefs about the moral life of man, the doctrine further states that it should be the aim of political action to maximize as far as possible what is called negative freedom. This notion implies that there are limits beyond which no one should be permitted, for any reason, to invade the freedom of the individual even if such an intrusion is deemed to be in his own best interests. Negative freedom is contrasted with positive freedom where the concern is more with the conditions of freedom than with the freedom itself; with the real possibility of attaining some ideal or good. This is the notion implicit in most paternalistic, socialist and revolutionary politics; and it can, according to its critics, lead to the idea of forcing others to do something they may not want to do, because someone in authority decides it is for their own or another's good.

But, while these concepts are distinct, it is freely admitted that there must be a dialogue between positive and negative freedom, since it is accepted that negative freedom is not an absolute. Thus there are certain kinds of actions, for example, slavery, murder or fraud, which should not be permitted. But when they are forbidden we must call a spade a spade, and say that we are limiting people's freedom to act in that way. According to the theory, the greatest source of moral and political confusion is to re-define these limitations into some other sense of that word as the proponents of positive freedom tend to do.

Behind this notion of pluralism and the concept of freedom which it implies, lies an image of the lone, subjectively free, autonomous individual who knows what he wants and is generally capable of making a rational decision as to how best achieve it. He is rational enough too to surrender such freedom as may be necessary for his purposes. But in principle he would like total freedom to follow wherever his desires and wants lead him. There is also, in a somewhat paradoxical way, an analogue of Rousseau's notion of the natural goodness of man. The average individual is a decent sort of

---

questions, especially when imposed by Church or State. But he is emphatic that we must accept some values as universal or near universal if the concept 'human' is to have any meaning at all. His position has been described as a strong (radical) version of liberalism because of his great stress on *negative* liberty, with a consequent downgrading of political action. The theory should not be confused with the contemporary debate about 'the enforcement of morals' as exemplified in the Hart-Devlin controversy. There is of course a theory of law implicit in Berlins' position and it is a negative one in the tradition of Hobbes and Bentham: law is simply a restriction on liberty. There are three steps in Berlins' argument. First, he asserts that negative liberty is an 'ultimate value'. Second, the doctrine of a 'pluralism of values' is offered as an argument to show the propriety of negative freedom. Third, negative freedom is destroyed to some extent by every legal constraint: freedom and constraint are contradictory opposites.

person who is usually concerned about the moral character of his actions and who, if given the freedom, will normally choose in a responsible way.

Perhaps the most important point of contrast with political pluralism is that moral pluralism does not entail any specific theory of the state or any particular form of political structure. In principle, an autocratic regime could provide a greater degree of negative freedom than could a democratic socialist society. But it does allow that greater participation in decision-making by individuals in all that concerns them is more likely to ensure those forms of negative freedom which they cherish most. In general it can be said that a society is free to the extent that it realizes negative freedom for its members.[7]

A CIVILIZING FORCE

It must be said that the appeal to pluralism in one or other of its forms has been a powerful force for civilizing our attitudes and relationships to each other. Where accepted, it has helped to enlarge cultural, religious and moral freedom but it has also created a great deal of injustice. Most states seek to accommodate as far as possible within their legal framework, the varying moral and religious attitudes of the defined groups which exist within their boundaries. In practice, most groups succeed in getting legal acceptance for their position, provided it is not seen by the majority as outrageous or shocking. Thus, for example, in most Western democracies, homosexuality has been removed from the criminal law; so too divorce has been permitted on the grounds of moral pluralism. The general

7. Nineteenth-century liberals feared that the spread of democracy would lead to the 'tyranny of numbers' and to the 'rejection of aristocratic values'. Rouseau was, and still remains for many liberals, and especially for Berlin, the chief enemy of negative freedom. This is partly because equality has never been an important value for liberals, whereas for Rouseau it was central to any theory of freedom and justice. One of the few *pluralist* writers who sought to keep equality as a central value in his system was J. Dewey, the American philosopher. He went beyond the English pluralists in asserting the need for positive state action if equality, justice and even democracy itself were to be attained: he rejected totally the *umpire* notion of the state. In spirit he was much nearer to Rousseau than he was to the English pluralists or indeed to the negative liberals. Today most liberal parties or movements believe in a large measure of positive state action in the interests of justice. Hence we speak of positive liberalism. Social Democratic parties tend to fall into this category of liberalism and normally they are committed also to a strong sense of moral pluralism in what is called the area of private morality. Some of these groups are also committed to a version of political pluralism.

approach seems to be that where there is a strong divergence of views about the morality of an action, the state should not criminalize such action or should de-criminalize it where it has been illegal before.

But it is clear that the degree to which the principle of pluralism is applied, depends to a great extent on attitudes towards the issues involved. Western democracies have been generous to what we might call religious, cultural and moral minorities but they have tolerated a great deal of injustice in terms of wealth, welfare, incomes, wages and other social categories.

LIMITS TO OUR PLURALIST SENSIBILITIES

It is clear then that at the heart of the pluralist ideal there is a paradox. On the one hand it is seen as the defender of the person against the group or of the groups against the pervading power of the state. On the other hand, it can justify the crudest forms of selfish behaviour on the part of some individuals or groups. Thus trade unions, employers' groups, pressure groups of all kinds can give a specious respectability to very selfish behaviour by invoking the principle of pluralism. The reason is quite simply that the pluralist principle is too obsessed with state power and too little concerned with the many forms of real power which individuals and groups can wield over others. Its stress on the value of the subordinate group and its suspicion of state power are used selectively in the interests of particular individuals and groups. As a result they are allowed, if they have the power and the influence, to elevate a particular interpretation of liberty above most other values.

It is clear, then, that other sorts of considerations need to be brought into focus whenever we discuss serious issues; and of course we do use other criteria all the time. We will not allow any one group to oppress another in some obvious, violent or shocking way.[8] Thus many of those who use the principle to argue against the referendum would refuse to use it in a similar sort of debate about pornography or child molestation or wife battering or paedophilia. But again many others would refuse to use it in regard to some or all of the following social and economic issues: education, social welfare, the creation of wealth, free collective bargaining, etc. These, the argument goes, are too important issues to be left to individuals or groups.

There are limits, then, to our pluralist sensibilities; but these limits derive more from our selfish concerns and our sense of shock or

8. One might ask whether, in this country, we allow the settled community to oppress itinerants or whether we allow itinerants to oppress the settled community.

horror at a particular kind of situation than from any clear, moral convictions or concern about their goodness. In general it can be said that we all agree to use the principle provided the result does not impinge too much on our own personal interest.

NOT A SURE GUIDE TO JUSTICE

Clearly then, the principle of pluralism isn't a very sure guide to justice in a society, and has within it the seeds of great injustice. As a guide to judging public policy it is seriously defective. While it has made invaluable contributions in limiting the intrusion of the state into the lives of persons and groups in some areas, it has also allowed destructive power of various kinds to remain in the hands of individuals and groups with very unpleasant consequences for others.

The reason for this is that the principle is accepted mostly as a guide to policy only in democratic societies. Built into its application, therefore, we have all the weaknesses of democracy. In particular, there is the inevitable tendency of counting heads to determine what is good or evil; and there are all the inequalities in power and the ability to influence government decisions which are an acknowledged feature of all our Western democratic societies.

Indeed Western democracies might best be characterized as an attempt to wed statism and pluralism in such a way that the wants and desires of those who wield most power are sufficiently fulfilled to win their allegiance to the state and its policies, thus guaranteeing peace and harmony. In such a context everything is permissible in principle; and we know only too well that Western democracies both originated and perpetrated many great evils with the tacit approval of its members. When pluralism and statism come together, there is a kind of 'live and let live' policy between the protagonists for power. It works well provided the limits which specify their respective interests are maintained. To say it works well is not to say that it works in the interest of justice or fairness or equality or goodness or even of civilization. What passes as progress and civilization, where the principle of pluralism is used to judge policy, is in many cases little more than selective barbarism.

LIMITS TO WHAT THE STATE TOLERATES

Is it possible, then, to specify any limits to the application of the principle of pluralism within a democratic society? We have already referred to the fact that almost everybody will have their own set of limits based on their own vision of life and their sense of horror; and we have said that the principle itself allows for appeal to other values where there is real conflict. But, taking the nature of the state and the person into account, is it possible to specify cases or principles where the principle of pluralism cannot be used to justify certain actions on the part of individuals and groups? Are there any actions or situations which the state must not tolerate no matter who or how many people think otherwise? If, for example, we could say that the state, in failing to prevent a certain action, was abnegating its most fundamental responsibility, then perhaps we might have some criteria. But it is impossible to give a theoretical answer to this question because the principle of pluralism would be invoked against it.

All one can do is protest and say that there must be such limits. Certainly, most people will agree that any direct attack on innocent life would be of such a kind. Once again the principle of pluralism intrudes its head when we come to the definition of innocent life. And within the context of a democratic society, this means that the state will inevitably opt for such considerations as peace and harmony rather than challenge a particularly strong group demanding freedom in the area concerned. The result is always a rather mish-mash of moral attitudes and views towards state policy.

Thus we get a situation where people would be appalled if the state were to permit slavery or torture or great poverty, and would be equally appalled if the state were to ban abortion. On the other hand, we can find people who would be immediately opposed to abortion and yet can accept extreme poverty, gross inequality and many other forms of violence against the person. Oppression is no less oppression because it does not originate from the state. The moral character of a society is revealed just as much by what we permit to be done to some of our members as by what we forbid others to do.

Quite clearly, we are all selective in our moral principles and in our attitudes to the state and our own interests. But the principle of pluralism justifies us in hanging on, in fighting for what we regard as our moral convictions and freedom, by which we mean the freedom to act as we see fit without let or hindrance from others. On the other hand, we all want the state to be in some way a protector of each one of us against what we regard as a violation of our persons. And to do this we recognize its power to coerce us in various ways. Most states accept this role. But it is a sad fact that the measure of their interest in the individual is determined by the significance of that individual for the state itself or for those who wield power within it. Hence the vast array of what we might call negative groups, such as the poor, the uneducated, the unprivileged, the hungry.

It is indeed a rare thing for any state to choose a certain line of action or policy because it is good in itself. Even the present referendum, seen from the point of view of the state, looks very much like a typical 'political' act, i.e. one entered into because of its significance for getting, or for holding power. Or it can be seen as a standard response to what might be called the democratic process. In a world where there is inequality of power and influence, the principle of pluralism can quite literally be a deadly weapon in the hands of some of us. On the other hand, when the principle of pluralism is not a guiding spirit in shaping the policy of any society, then many people will experience institutional violence.

In the present debate on abortion, we find the concept of pluralism frequently used in one or other of its derivatives. It is stated for example that Ireland is a pluralist society. What is meant by this is never clearly stated. Does it mean that Ireland is a society which is committed to the ideal of political pluralism, i.e. a society which places great importance on the person and on natural or voluntary social groupings, whether cultural or religious, and seeks to diminish the influence of the state and its inevitable control of life? Or does it mean that the people or government in Ireland are committed to enlarging the areas of negative freedom for individuals?

As for the first sense of pluralism, we can scarcely apply that description to Ireland, North or South, or indeed to any European democratic state. Today we expect the state to play fairy godmother in many areas of our life, and look to it to solve our problems. In that sense neither Ireland nor any Western democracy is truly pluralist. As for the moral sense of pluralism, it is difficult to say that it is an accepted principle of social and political policy in Ireland. We tend to see our problems in black and white terms, and we believe that an ultimate reconciliation of conflicting values is possible. We are suspicious of any proposal to extend the area of negative freedom to those actions which most Irish people regard as evil.

IRISH SOCIETY DE FACTO PLURALIST IN MORALS

Probably what most people mean when they say Ireland is pluralist, is that there is now a de facto pluralism, of religion, culture and values, or a moral pluralism. In other words, Irish society is factually a plural society because it is composed of groups whose defining features differ substantially in all or some of these ways. This is scarcely new, since it is highly unlikely that Ireland was ever a homogeneous society, even though we may have pretended to be so. Abstracting from some limited areas of agreement, it is fair to use the factual description of pluralist in religious, cultural, moral, social and political terms. But it was a pluralism without any commitment to the pluralist idea or principle.

Returning to the present debate, we must assume that we are being asked to regard Irish society as a de facto pluralist society in regard to the morality of abortion. Secondly, we are being asked to apply the principle of pluralism in one or other sense unspecified, in order to assess the moral and juridical value of the proposed referendum.

It is important to stress this point, for the principle is not being invoked to pass judgement on the moral character of abortion, as is sometimes suggested. It is precisely the clash of judgements that justify the invocation of the principle; it is the presumed uncertainty as to how best to reconcile the conflict of interests involved.

It is argued by those who invoke the principle of pluralism that it would be an injustice (i.e. an unfair infringement of their moral liberty) to those individuals or groups who favour abortion as a permissible and sometimes necessary action, to make it unconstitutional. This position is advocated both by those who regard abortion as a morally justifiable action and by some of those who reject it as such. The supposition on both sides, however, must be that the most desirable situation in terms of the principle of pluralism so understood, is one in which abortion is no longer illegal either constitutionally or in terms of the criminal law.

There are, of course, others who reject abortion and accept the present condition of criminalization of the act, and who yet reject the referendum for reasons other than the principle of pluralism, for example, reasons connected with their understanding of what a constitution ought to be. For these people a constitution is a fundamental law outlining the general features of how a society wishes to govern itself. Because of its historical character, they want the document to be otherwise as general as possible, thus removing the need to tamper with it too frequently while still allowing other forms of legislation to adjust to changing needs and times. For these people, their opposition to the referendum is based on their definition of a constitution, and this is a perfectly valid position to hold.

CONSTITUTION SPECIFIES IDEALS AND VALUES

However, it needs to be said that our present constitution is not of this kind, that it does prescribe ideals and values and not just the juridical framework. Moreover, it specifies a certain hierarchy of values about which there can be arguments. But its silence on the rights of the unborn child may need to be challenged just as its implicit rejection of the illegitimate child does. In a word, while we have the kind of constitution we have, it seems right and proper to some to challenge it on any issues about which people feel deeply as to their presence in or absence from the constitution. Precisely because constitutions are historical documents, they will need change in detail and fundamentals, and that is what the process of amendment is for. A constitution which would never need amendment would be either Utopian or so empty of content as to be useless. This precise criticism of the referendum is more appropriately directed against the constitution itself than against the proposed referendum which it makes possible.

In the last analysis, then, the argument comes down to our moral attitude to abortion and to our attitudes to the function of law and more particularly the function of the constitution as it is now or might be in the future.

STATE MUST PROTECT VALUES

If anyone sees abortion in the same context as torture or rape or slavery or wife battering or degrading poverty, and believes that it is the task of the constitution to protect our ideals on these matters, one might say that they have a duty to ensure that such ideals are stated in the constitution and perhaps reflected in the criminal law. For them the state has the task of protecting these values even if it means coercion of some people. In other words, abortion is the kind of thing that requires the ultimate legal sanction. It cannot be justified anymore than can torture or murder by invoking the principle of pluralism. And indeed this is how many people see it.

To describe their action as sectarian, even if their beliefs are derived from religious conviction, is simply an abuse of language. Indeed, the very principle of pluralism itself can be invoked in their favour. What they are doing is trying to protect a weak and defenceless group of people being killed by those stronger than they. If one believes in the principle of pluralism, one must believe in it for all, else it simply becomes the morality of might is right, and justice is the interests of the stronger. Pluralism does not dispense us from concern for others whether as individuals or groups.

Of course, this use of the principle assumes that the unborn child belongs to the very same category of being human as the rest of us, and that killing him/her is in principle the same sort of action as killing any other person. If, then, to seek to defend the rights of others against those who wish to legalize their killing or to weaken whatever protection the law might give them, is to be regarded as sectarian, then all concern for justice is sectarian. Many Catholics throughout the world who are fighting on behalf of deprived and oppressed groups of people and who seek to right that aggression by influencing government and changing the laws of the land, are equally sectarian if their views or motivations derive from religious convictions.

A MORAL STANCE IS NOT SECTARIAN

It is, indeed, unwise for any democrat to use that word against his opponents, since it undercuts the very basis of his own claims to speak and influence the life of the community. From the present debate, it would seem that one can only be sectarian if one happens to be a Catholic and advocates legislation on some issue. It isn't apparently sectarian for Protestants or humanists or for atheists or trade unionists to propose legislation or to oppose the referendum even though that opposition derives from the ethos of their group.

Whether people favour or oppose a particular piece of legislation, they are taking a moral stance whether as individuals or groups and if people insist on using the term sectarian, neither side of this debate has a monopoly of that attitude. One doesn't have to have a church, a pope or bishop to belong to a sect or to act in a sectarian fashion. There are secular as well as religious sects; and their members are no less immune to sectarianism, which I take to mean the desire on the part of one group to impose its views about behaviour and social organization on others, and that because of a genuine belief that the value in question is one of great importance.[9] The most sectarian groups in the western world are the communist parties, and for many of their members, it derives from sincerely held views.

---

9. Some people use the word in a pejorative sense, suggesting that malice of some kind is implied whenever people criticize or act in the light of religious or moral convictions. Such use is much more appropriate when groups, who exercize a lot of power, use it to advance their own selfish interests. An attempt by the Vincent de Paul Society to use their power as a group to obtain a fairer share for the poor and deprived can hardly be compared with the use of power by a trade union, for example, or by an employers' group to obtain a larger slice of the national cake.

IS FOETAL LIFE HUMAN LIFE?

Those who favour the referendum do so because they regard abortion as evil, in the same sort of way that murder or torture are, and because they believe that foetal life is just as sacred as is any other stage of human life, and that we should protect it as strongly as possible. Thus, for them there are very definite limits to using the principle of pluralism to make judgements on public policy. Quite simply, for such people neither considerations of the freedom of the individual nor even the unity or harmony of the state itself, can justify the state, either killing or allowing others to kill innocent human life. For the state to do either would be tantamount to forfeiting all claims to respect from people who think this way.

Those who seek to legalize abortion on demand, and there are many involved in this debate for whom that is the ultimate goal, would deny the very premise of the last few paragraphs. For them foetal life is quite simply not human life, and, if it can be so described in some sense or other, then it hasn't the same status as those already born. In effect, killing foetal life is not in any real sense killing a person or a human being: It is the killing (yes, it must be described as killing) of some indeterminate, indescribable form of life. Some would perhaps describe it as vegetable or animal or just a blob but they cannot, when they so regularly kill it, allow themselves describe it as human and still claim to be concerned about the sanctity or dignity of human life. For such people the question of respecting or protecting foetal life does not arise since there is nothing there that merits such response from others. Such people regard abortion, at least from the moral point of view, as akin to removing an appendix or cutting one's toenails; or, on their more frequently used analogy, to the spontaneous loss of fertilised ova. The future of the foetus is usually decided by asking the mother to answer a few questions that have nothing to do with the child. By so defining foetal life, the argument about the referendum or any other form of prohibition on abortion is simply defined out of court.

RECOGNIZING A REAL CLASH OF VALUES

There are others who wish to see abortion decriminalised but who still regard it as the necessary, but regrettable killing of a human being in some sense or other. They find justification in the necessities which create the situation. For these people there is a real clash of values and they feel that they must or can be reconciled in the interests of the adult person. For them the proposed and indeed existing legislation imposes on the person one particular resolution of the conflict which in circumstances may seem grossly unfair to him/her. These people tend to fall back on the lack of certitude about the real status of foetal life. Perhaps it is not a person in a full sense; and that while one is killing human life, it is quite different from killing an adult person. Hence they feel strongly entitled to invoke the principle of moral pluralism to guarantee their freedom to resolve the conflict as they best understand it. For them it is indeed a matter of freedom of conscience. These people are also bearing genuine moral witness to the problem of abortion and their views must be given serious consideration by those who oppose abortion.

Clearly, these are morally sensitive people and they are saying something not just about the conflict which abortion raises for them but about moral conflicts in general, and how we should see the role of law in areas of personal moral conflict.[10] They are entitled to feel aggrieved when others seek to prevent them acting as they see fit. They must also try to understand why others feel morally compelled to resort to legislation to prevent them so acting. It is essential for those who oppose abortion to listen to such people, and perhaps to create dialogue between their different perspectives. They may each come to have a clearer understanding of their respective positions about the wisdom or unwisdom of bringing secular law into this particular area of life.

Some may see it as more destructive than creative of morality in the long run, because law is a rough instrument in this area. And what is seen as justice by one may be experienced as injustice by others. Yet this is the human condition and people cannot ignore their moral sensitivities even though their actions may hurt others. Concern for one set of values will, as we have said, lead to the negation of others which are also cherished. Whatever one may think of the doctrine of indirect abortion, it should be stressed that it was developed by people who had this kind of moral awareness and sensitivity. It was not, as some suggest, a dishonest effort to avoid the worst consequences of giving foetal life an absolute value.

---

10. Among this group of people there are clearly some, who view abortion with the same horror as do those who propose the referendum, and yet in the name of freedom of conscience cannot accept criminalization of the act. Such people, on the contrary, demand that the state should protect this moral freedom from majorities and pressure groups.

ATTITUDES TO HUMAN LIFE

The real value of this debate is that it challenges us all to look at our basic moral vision and in particular our attitude to human life in general. Basically there are two sorts of vision.

One sees human life as a spectrum from the moment of conception to death. At every point in the spectrum life is equally sacred. Any violation of that life is precluded no matter what the justification. The high point of this moral vision can be expressed in the age old dictum that it is better to suffer injustice than to commit it, no matter how lofty the motive. The application of the adage, of course, begs a lot of questions. What it does tell us is that we should be prepared to die rather than take the slightest risk of doing evil. And some mothers did just that in the past. We always risk evil whenever another human life is injured or degraded by us in any way. This fact cautions us not to presume on the justice of our action.

This vision is, of course, a harrowing one and calls for courage beyond the normal. This kind of courage few of us have. For those who live by it, anything else is compromise. For those who do not share it, it is a Utopian dream and too hard for human nature to accept. Most of the great thinkers were willing to modify it in the interests of various values. It is the morality of turning the other cheek and refusing to lift a hand against another lest in doing so, one may commit evil. Within this vision, appeal to law as a source of goodness or justice has little place because law is always suspect of being on the side of the strong. To invoke law is simply to shift the focus from personal use of force to the institutional use of it; it is then to enlarge the risk of evil. This does not imply any sort of quietism or indifference to social or personal injustice. Rather this attitude will find its expression in the passion of a Socrates or a John the Baptist who will expose evil in all its aspects whether it be the tyranny of the great or the ambition and greed of the small and who will also cherish all aspects of human life because of their reverence for the mystery of life itself.

The second vision is not as absolutist as the first. It tends to look for balance and indeed compromise in moral situations. Its basic stand-point concerns the freedom and dignity of the person and always in the terms in which he himself will assess them. There is an assumption that the function of morality is to serve the interests of the person in the best sense of that word, though interest may not always be decided in the best sense. And what pertains to morality is also decided by the individual. There is in this vision an ambivalent attitude to the state. On the one hand it is there to serve the interests of the person, while on the other, it must give the individual maximum freedom to seek those interests in the way he judges best. It is accepted that in the working out of this dialectic certain things will be done which may not be good for all; some may have to suffer for what is called the common good. Where there are differences about certain issues, each one claims his freedom to do his own thing. The only limits accepted are one's own moral attitudes and the legal limits imposed by the state. These latter are not of great moral import, and flouting them is permissible so long as one does not suffer for it.

In general, it is a 'live and let-live' philosophy, so long as my freedom and my privileges are not infringed and so long as I do not infringe the freedom of those who could retaliate against me. Life has to be lived in the real world, and it is a sad fact of that world that we may have to do or permit the doing of things we would in our heart of hearts rather not have to do. Thus most of us would rather if we didn't have prisons or capital punishment, but it is sad that our security demands them. So, too, most of us would rather that abortion was never necessary but it is a proved fact of life that it is in certain circumstances. We did not make the world; but we have to live in it and do our best to live a decent life with as much respect for others and as little recourse to evil as possible. However, if you want an omelette you must break eggs and there are many situations in life where we must do evil small or great. It is not we who are to blame for the hangman's work. It was the criminal who made the hangman a necessary feature of our society. So too, it is poverty or a brutal husband or a justified week-end of self-enjoyment or the gossiping neighbours who cause abortions to take place. The individual man or woman involved in the abortion is simply a victim of circumstances. It is an ultimate remedy for an unpleasant situation created mostly by others for me. Or again business is business; and that means that, if I am to survive, I must behave like my competitors. Too bad, some people will suffer as a result. But that is how the world is and we can do little about it.

In this way of seeing things, there is a kind of moral fatalism; but of course none of us can live with that and so we elevate these unpleasant necessities into a kind of moral code. Only that way can we keep our sense of integrity and achieve our goals. We may not be fully masters of our fate, but the highest moral aim is to achieve it as nearly as possible, no matter what the cost.

It seems fairly clear that the modern drift to statism will only be tolerated on condition that maximum freedom of the personal moral kind is allowed. The subtle encroachment of the state into our lives can only be bought by a parallel extension of the area of personal freedom and choice in matters about which the state can be neutral.

Thus we have the illusion of progress and civilization; but to a great extent it is a delicate balance of conflicting interests. We will fight for baby seals but not for unborn babies, or a fairer distribution of wealth, or care for the old and deprived. The obsession which many have with the nuclear hazard runs hand in hand with great indifference to the millions who are starving and dying or being deliberately killed.

Inevitably, then, there is little place within this vision for the politically and socially weak. Quite simply a person must do what he must do to survive, even if survival is maintaining a pretty luxurious level of life involving the deprivation of others. And we expect the state both to legalize this behaviour and to provide us also with the means which give us the freedom to engage in it.[11]

There is no easy answer then, as to whether the proposed amendment is morally good or bad. At best there are strong indications on one side or the other, depending on how one sees the function of law and constitutions in regard to justice.

But whatever the answer about the moral character of the referendum, we should not let ourselves be confused about the real nature of abortion. In some ways it is far easier to present the case for it than against it, and it is easier to move people towards accepting it than rejecting it. That is the story of its growth everywhere. For that reason we may well look back and see that it was very unwise to start this campaign at all. When all the words have flowed and the ink is dry, it is highly probable that more people will favour abortion than did before the debate, and that public opinion will have shifted somewhat towards accepting abortion as part of our medical services. The best 'reflectors' of public opinion are the young who absorb it unconsciously, and already many of them are ambivalent on the issue.

11. Far too little attention is paid to the coercive power of administrative law. Our family law is a good example. Our tax sytem can also be coercive not only when it is unfair, but also when public money is used to fund programmes that some may regard as immoral. Abortion or contraception provided by the welfare services could be experienced as such by some people. The Americans are much more aware of this aspect of coercion. The principle of pluralism works both ways. Or again, our ambivalence about the Irish language creates situations where both groups can experience coercion.

But the fact that the question arose at all marks a new phase in the moral consciousness of the Irish people. We are re-defining not just our attitudes to foetal life but to human life in general and the framework of values by which we set limits to our actions. In so far as we invoke the principle of moral pluralism, we are opting for greater moral freedom for the individual. Whether this will yield a more or less caring society or bring with it a larger measure of self-assertion by the strong at the expense of the weak, cannot be determined now. If the amendment is carried, it will not stop the abortion trail to England. But it was never meant to do that anyway. It will simply stave off the day when in Ireland killing unborn babies will be part of the daily roster in our hospitals. But for how long?

In a democracy where public morality is the reflection of the wants and desires of the majority or the strong vocal minority, no law can guarantee the answer desired by those who propose the amendment. Ireland will almost inevitably go down the abortion road simply because there is too little reverence for life here, and there are few signs of change in our attitudes. We have glorified, and still glorify the killing of people, defined out of innocence, because they hinder or refuse to serve some personal or group cause. It is a habit which, once acquired, is difficult to reverse. To say these things is neither prophecy nor despair. Neither will the advent of abortion prove conclusively that either side was wrong about the morality of the referendum. Neither the failure of the one nor the success of the other will fully explain that development. Change arises within the hearts of individuals, and when enough people believe in or want something, the law tends to follow suit in a democracy. Whatever the outcome, some even among those who oppose abortion will experience a sense of moral regression.

If the referendum is defeated, the contours of a new area of negative freedom will have been delineated even if not finally settled, and for many this is a sign of progress leading to social maturity and a development not to be bartered for an unnecessary and unrealistic attempt to protect the unborn child. Others will see it quite simply as giving people the freedom to destroy all freedom for other human beings.

If the referendum succeeds, some will see this as establishing the claims of the unborn child to be a human being and refusing to allow others the freedom to kill it. Others will see it as a new curb on freedom and an unjustifiable intrusion by the state into their lives.

The former will see it as protecting the child and bringing honour to the state. The latter will see it as bringing odium on the law while doing nothing real to protect the child.

The dilemma is not new: It derives from the nature of goodness and the moral character of man and it imposes on us the need to make painful and difficult choices between values that may be equally cherished by us but cannot both be realized as we would wish. How we resolve these dilemmas in our personal lives will depend on our moral character which, in Christian terms, may be anywhere along a spectrum ranging from the vicious to the holy. How we resolve them as a people will depend not only on our personal fibre, but also on our moral understanding of freedom and law. Camus summed it up brilliantly in one of his aphorisms: 'Whoever greatly loves a value is thereby an enemy of freedom. Whoever loves freedom above all either negates values or else adopts them only temporarily.'

The Need for a Constitutional Amendment

WILLIAM BINCHY*

The debate about the forthcoming constitutional referendum is, first, a legal one: whether there is a problem with our present legal protection of the right to life of the unborn and, if so, whether an amendment to the Constitution is necessary to resolve it. But the debate also raises important questions of a broader political nature, concerning such important issues as the solution to diversity of moral viewpoints in a society, the relevance of religious perspectives and their relationship to the protection of human rights. In this paper I will attempt to address these questions in turn.

THE LEGAL BACKGROUND

The past decade has witnessed a general judicial trend throughout the world in favour of abortion and against giving legal recognition to the right to life of the unborn.[1] In Ireland we are perhaps most familiar with the constitutional developments on these lines in the United States, but throughout much of Europe a similar trend is apparent. Moreover, international conventions for the protection of human rights and freedoms increasingly are being interpreted in a manner that gives little recognition to the right of life of the unborn. A lawyer with experience and understanding of international trends would therefore approach the Irish legal position in its proper context. Our law does not operate in a complete cultural vacuum; to some extent it is influenced by developments elsewhere and, in relation to the unborn, these developments are almost uniformly unfavourable.

Turning specifically to the legal position in Ireland, let us first look briefly at the general structural background.

* William Binchy, Barrister-at-Law, Research Counsellor, The Law Reform Commission. This paper is written in an entirely personal capacity and seeks to represent only the personal views of the author.

1. See Michel, *Abortion and International Law: The Status and Possible Extension of Women's Right to Privacy*, 20 J. of Family L. 241 (1981), Lyon & Bennett, *Abortion — A Question of Human Rights*, 12 Family L. 47 (1982).

Our fundamental law is the Constitution, enacted in 1937.[2] All legislation, whether enacted before or after 1937, is subject to the Constitution. If any legislative provision is not consistent with the Constitution it has no legal effect. The High Court and the Supreme Court have the sole responsibility to determine whether legislation is or is not consistent with the Constitution. If the Court strikes down the legislation, then the legislation immediately ceases to have any legal effect, even in cases where it was enacted with the full approval of all members of the Oireachtas and of the electorate as a whole.

THE LEGAL PROBLEM

There is a serious problem in relation to the rights of the unborn. The present legislation prohibiting abortion could be challenged at any time on the basis that it offends against the Constitution. Would such a challenge be successful? Obviously we cannot know the answer to this question with certainty until the case has been decided, but several factors give rise to concern that the challenge could well succeed. First, the Constitution gives no explicit protection to the unborn. From the standpoint of the unborn this is unquestionably a bad start. As we have seen, international experience indicates that courts throughout the world have been slow to read protection for the unborn into constitutions and conventions when this has not been done in the exact words of the basic document.[3] If there is no *explicit* protection for the unborn in the Constitution, perhaps there is some form of *implicit* protection? Lawyers have combed the Constitution but have not come up with impressive evidence that the unborn are adequately protected by some implicit provision in the Constitution. All that have been found are two *obiter dicta* by Mr Justice Walsh.[4] *Obiter dicta* are passages in a judgment not essential to the holding of the case, which bind no judge in any subsequent decision, not even the judge who delivered them. Mr Justice Walsh is, of course, a jurist of international eminence, but he would be the first to agree that these *obiter dicta* cannot afford adequate protection for the unborn against constitutional attack.

There are further grounds for concern about the adequacy of the present legal protection for the right to life of the unborn. The only

2. Cf. J. Kelly, *The Irish Constitution* (1980).
3. See Michel, *supra*, fn. 1, at 251ff.
4. Cf. *McGee v. A.G.* [1974] I.R. 284, at 312 (Sup. Ct.) 1973, *G. v. An Bord Uchtala* [1980] I.R. 32, at 69 (Sup. Ct.).

constitutional reference to a right to life is contained in Article 40, Section 3, as follows:

> 1° The State guarantees in its laws to respect, and, as far as practicable, by its laws to defend and vindicate the personal rights of the citizen.

> 2° The State shall, in particular, by its laws protect as best it may from unjust attack and, in the case of injustice done, vindicate the life, person, good name, and property rights of every citizen.

It is patently clear that this sole constitutional reference to a right to life refers *only* to 'citizens'. Moreover, the Constitution specifically says that citizenship shall be determined in accordance with law. Article 9, Section 3, sub-section (2) provides that

> The future acquisition and loss of Irish nationality and citizenship shall be determined in accordance with law.

That 'law' is contained in Section 6(1) of the *Irish Nationality and Citizenship Act 1956* which provides that

> [e]very person born in Ireland is an Irish citizen from birth.

Subsection (2) of the same section provides that

> [e]very person is an Irish citizen if his father or mother was an Irish citizen at the time of that person's birth or becomes an Irish citizen, under subsection (1) or would be an Irish citizen under that subsection if alive at the passing of this Act.

Since, therefore, citizenship cannot be acquired until birth, it appears to follow that:

1. the unborn are explicitly excluded from being citizens, and therefore
2. the unborn are specifically excluded from any Constitutional protection of a right to life under Article 40.

There is, however, a straw to cling to in favour of the view that non-citizens may rely on Article 40.3. In *The State (Nicolaou) v. An Bord*

Uchtala,[5] the High Court were split on this question, and in the Supreme Court, Mr Justice Walsh stated:

> The High Court judgments rested in part upon the fact that the appellant is not a citizen of Ireland. This Court expressly reserves for another and more appropriate case consideration of the effect of non-citizenship upon the interpretation of the Articles in question and also the right of a non-citizen to challenge the validity of an Act of the Oireachtas having regard to the provisions of the Constitution.[6]

That statement at least does not close the door finally on the argument that non-citizens may claim the protection of Article 40, but of course it falls well short of positive support or endorsement of the view that the unborn, though not citizens fall within the scope of Article 40.3.[7]

5. [1966] I.R. 567.
6. *Id.,* at 645.
7. Professor John Kelly (*The Irish Constitution,* 374 (1980)) notes that '[t]he questions whether non-citizens may rely on constitutional guarantees expressed to be for the benefit of "citizens" has not . . . been decided . . .' Referring to the *Nicolaou* reservation, Professor Kelly comments (at 375):

> As, however, the personal rights of Art. 40.3. have been repeatedly said by the Courts to be 'natural' and antecedent to the Constitution, it is hard to see how non-citizens can be prevented from relying on them.

Addressing the specific issue raised in *Nicolaou*, Professor Robert Heuston notes that:

> The phrase 'of the citizen' has given rise to difficulties [in Article 40.3] and elsewhere throughout the fundamental rights Articles. . . . The Supreme Court seems to be uncertain whether the constitutional guarantees protect aliens, [*State (Nicolaou) v. Attorney General* [1966] I.R. 567, at 599, 645] although in one case on the matter (*Re Singer*) [97 I.L.T.R. 130 (1963)] in which the issue might have arisen, counsel for the State expressly disclaimed any reliance on it. Clearly it would be very embarrassing for the Court, especially since the State has joined the European Economic Community, to be obliged to hold that an alien was not entitled to the same degree of protection as a citizen. On the other hand, simply as a matter of interpretation of words, it is very difficult to see how the word 'citizen' can be held to mean 'any person whether a citizen or an alien'. [*Personal Rights Under the Irish Constitution,* 11 U. British Columbia L. Rev. 294, at 304 (1977).]

Of course the non-citizenship of the unborn raises different issues than that of the alien but, in view of the very specific provisions in both the Constitution and the legislation relating to elegibility for citizenship, a similar difficulty arises as to how and why the unborn should be entitled to overcome their specific exclusion from constitutional protection.

But the dangers for the unborn are not limited to the fact that the Constitution affords them neither explicit nor clear implicit protection: a more radical threat has appeared. Our Constitution could be interpreted as conferring a broad right to abortion on demand, based on a woman's 'right to privacy'[8] in respect of procreation. Such a right, if recognized by the courts, would be a constitutionally protected 'personal right'. Under Article 40.3.1° of the Constitution, the state guarantees 'in its laws to respect, and, so far as practicable, by its laws to defend and vindicate the personal rights of the citizen'. Some of these 'personal rights' are spelt out in Article 40.3.2°[9] but the question arose as to whether there might be other personal rights, not specifically mentioned in the Constitution. The answer came in 1965, in the case of *Ryan v. Attorney General*,[10] when the Supreme Court accepted for the first time that it was exclusively the function of the High Court and Supreme Court to ascertain and declare the unspecified personal rights protected by the Constitution. Thus the *court*, and not the legislature, is the first and final arbiter of the question.

Since *Ryan's* case, a wide spectrum of these unspecified personal rights has been documented by the courts.[11] Perhaps the most significant is the right to marital privacy recognized in *McGee v. Attorney General*,[12] in 1973. The Supreme Court in that case was clearly receptive to the United States Court decision of *Griswold v. Connecticut*,[13] in 1965, which has also formulated a right to marital

8. See generally Gerety, *Redefining Privacy*, 12 Harv. C.R.-C.L. Rev. 233 (1977), Huff, *Thinking Clearly About Privacy*, 55 Washington L. Rev. 777, at 785 ff. (1980), Richardson, *The Individual, the Family, and the Constitution: A Jurisprudential Perspective*, 55 N.Y.U.L. Rev. 1 (1980), Fisher, *The Case for Abortion: A Plea for Unrestrictive Laws*, 56 Women Lawyers Journal 95 (1970), Fugua, *Justice Harry A. Blackman: The Abortion Decision*, 34 Arkansas L. Rev. 376 (1980), Gavison, *Privacy and the Limits of Law*, 89 Yale L. J. 421 (1980).
9. Article 40.3.2° provides that:

> The State shall, in particular, by its laws protect as best it may from unjust attack and, in the case of injustice done, vindicate the life, person, good name, and property rights of every citizen.

10. [1965] I.R. 294 (Sup. Ct., affirming Kenny, J.).
11. Cf. Heuston, *Personal Rights under the Irish Constitution*, 11 U. British Columbia L. Rev. 294, at 313 (1977):

> The speed with which new unspecified rights can be recognised and enforced is startling.

12. [1974] I.R. 284 (Sup. Ct., 1973, reversing Murnaghan, J.).
13. 381 U.S. 479 (1965).

privacy. Yet within the short period of eight years,[14] the right to marital privacy in the United States had become[15] a right to procreative privacy entitling a woman to have what, in effect, amounts to 'abortion on demand'.

This is a source of urgent concern for Irish jurisprudence, since American constitutional law has had a considerable influence on Irish judges. As Mr Justice D'Arcy stated in a High Court decision[16] in 1982, 'decisions of the Supreme Court of the United States will always be received by this Court with the greatest of respect'.

No one can say with certainty how an Irish court would resolve the constitutional clash between the right to life of the unborn and the mother's right to privacy as a basis of a right to abortion.[17] What one can say with certainty is that the present constitutional position leaves the unborn at risk. An amendment is therefore necessary to

14. The important 'bridging' decision was *Eisenstadt v. Baird*, 405 U.S. 438 (1972). Cf. Smith, *The Constitution and Autonomy*, 60 Texas L. Rev. 175, at 189-190, 197 (1982).

15. In *Roe v. Wade*, 410 U.S. 113 (1973); see also *Doe v. Bolton*, 410 U.S. 179 (1973). The decision led to a flood of commentary. Among the more frequently-cited analyses are Ely, *The Wages of Crying Wolf: A Comment on Roe v. Wade*, 82 Yale L. J. 920 (1973), O'Meara, *The Court Decides a Non-Case*, [1973] Sup. Ct. Rev. 337, Goodman, Schoenbroad & Steavis, *Doe and Roe: Where Do We Go From Here?* 1 Women's Rts L. Reptr. 20 (1973), Healey, *Haunting Shadows from the Rubble of Roe's Right to Privacy*, 9 Suffolk U. L. Rev. 145 (1974), Satris, *Roe! Doe! Where Are You? The Effect of the Supreme Court's Abortion Decisions*, 7 U. Calif. Davis L. Rev. 432 (1974), Tribe, *The Supreme Court 1972 Term — Forward: Toward a Model of Roles in the Due Process of Life and Law*, 87 Harv. L. Rev. 1 (1973), Destro, *Abortion and the Constitution: The Need for a Life-Protective Amendment*, 63 Calif. L. Rev. 1250 (1975), Anon., *In Defense of Liberty: A Look at the Abortion Decisions*, 61 Georgetown L. J. 1559 (1973), Bryant, *State Legislation on Abortion after Roe v. Wade: Selected Constitutional Issues*, 2 Am. J. of L. & Med. 101 (1976), Heymann & Barzelay, *The Forest and the Trees: Roe v. Wade and Its Critics*, 53 Boston U. L. Rev. 765 (1973).

16. *O'Brien v. Stoutt*, High Ct., 5 March 1982 (1977 No. 3264P). See also *The State (Quinn) v. Ryan* [1965] I.R. 70, at (Sup. Ct., *per* Walsh, J.): 'In this State one would have expected that if the approach of any Court of final appeal of another State was to have been held up as an example for this Court to follow it would more appropriately have been the Supreme Court of the United States rather than the House of Lords'. One should not, of course, overstress this point. There have been cases in which the Irish courts have not followed United States precedents. The problem in relation to abortion is not that the American precendent *must* be followed here, but that it *may*. There is a doubt on the question and it is not proper that the right to life of the unborn should rest on a doubt.

17. See J. Kelly, *The Irish Constitution*, 374 (1980), O'Reilly, *Marital Privacy and Family Law*, 65 Studies 8 (1977), Binchy, *Marital Privacy and Family Law: A Reply to Mr O'Reilly*, 65 Studies 330 (1977), Casey, *The Development of Constitutional Law under Chief Justice Ó Dálaigh* [1978] Dublin U. L. J. 1, at 10.

ensure that the unborn no longer be exposed to this risk. If, as a society, we are opposed to abortion on demand, then it is only prudent that we ensure that our law gives effect to this policy.

It has been argued that a right to life for the unborn is not an appropriate subject for inclusion in a Constitution. I disagree. There is no other place to declare this right.

One line of thought[18] is that a constitution should declare very generally attitudes and aspirations of the community and place only very general limits on legislative power. But to regard the Irish Constitution in this light is to misunderstand its nature.

Whether we like it or not, our Constitution does not confine itself to general communal aspirations: on the contrary, as we have seen, it gives the courts (*and not the community*) the power to determine very specific and enforceable rights and obligations.

But we must remember that the community is entitled to have the last word. The community, when it passed the Constitution in the first place, gave the sole right to interpret it to the courts. The community is unquestionably entitled to give the courts guidance as to what the people think and to fill any loopholes which may appear from time to time. We did this recently in the case of adoption. It seems reasonable that we should do it in the case of life itself.

If our Constitution were of the vague type which some people mistakenly believe it to be, one could appreciate the argument that the Constitution should not include specific reference to the right to life of the unborn. But instead our Constitution is a powerful instrument. It is capable of being interpreted as conferring on citizens a right to abortion on demand: all that is necessary is one court decision.

In these circumstances, other expressions of concern for the attitudes and aspirations of the community regrettably miss the most important point and fail to understand the role of the courts in constitutional law. The abortion issue *already* has a constitutional dimension, whether or not the amendment becomes part of our law.

THE AMENDMENT AND PLURALISM

We now come to an issue that has received considerable attention in the debate and to which several other contributors to this book have adverted. It has been argued that a constitutional amendment would

18. Cf. Barden, *An Amendment We Can Do Without*, in M. Arnold & P. Kirby eds., *'The Abortion Referendum': The Case Against*, 50, at 52 (1982).

offend against principles of pluralism and that it should be rejected on this account.

The issue of abortion clearly involves questions of human rights and of social policy which transcend religious considerations. Whether a person subscribes to any particular religion or to none, he or she will be required, as a member of our society, to take a position on the basic human rights questions which the abortion issue involves. The case for a constitutional amendment is based squarely on the fact that the human rights of the unborn have become vulnerable to legal attack. But, it is argued by some persons opposing the amendment, certain religious denominations do not oppose the legalisation of abortion in some instances. Would not an amendment offend the consciences of members of these denominations?

The short answer to this line of argument can perhaps be given by an example. A two-year old girl is run over by a car and severely injured. She is in urgent need of a blood transfusion. Her parents, devout Jehovah's Witnesses, refuse their permission for the blood transfusion on religious grounds. The law in all countries will intervene and save the life of the child.[19] Who could argue that the law should instead defer to the parents' conscientious beliefs? Why should the answer be different if the little girl had not yet been born, but was nonetheless in need of a blood transfusion?[20] What principle would allow a pluralist solution in the latter, but not in the former, case?

Let us examine the pluralist thesis on abortion a little more closely. It does not seek to argue that *particular* attitudes towards abortion now held in various denominations are right or wrong: indeed its entire thrust is that the law should not select between differing views.

As it happens, the Protestant denominations, so far as they favour grounds for abortion, express themselves in moderate terms. For example, Mr McDowell, Joint Convenor of the Presbyterian Church's Government Committee, has emphasized that that Church does not want easy abortion: 'in fact we hardly want the possibility of abortion at all'. It is reasonable to assume that not all Irish Protestants would favour such a restrictive approach. Freedom of individual conscience on moral issues is at the heart of Protestant thinking.[21] The range of opinion on abortion is therefore likely to be

19. Cf. e.g. Wright & Linden, *Canadian Tort Law: Cases, Notes and Materials,* 96-97 (6th ed., 1975).
20. Cf. Wright & Linden, *supra,* at 96.
21. Cf. Rev. Peter Tarleton, *Violating Church of Ireland Freedom,* in M. Arnold & P. Kirby eds., *"The Abortion Referendum": The Case Against,* 45, at 46 (1982).

fairly extensive. In countries where abortion has already been legalised, some Protestant denominations support very liberal abortion laws[22] (although it should also be noted that other Protestant denominations are very strongly opposed to abortion[23] and their members are playing a leading role in pro-life organizations).

From the pluralist standpoint, what is significant about this wide spectrum of denominational attitudes towards abortion is that it extends as far as support for laws permitting abortion on demand. A pluralist approach to abortion must therefore accommodate attitudes more liberal towards abortion than have so far been expressed by various denominational spokesmen. We are entitled, therefore, to ask of those who articulate a pluralist position to be honest and frank in admitting that pluralism has some rather startling implications for abortion law. If pluralism requires that we permit abortion where the unborn child suffers from 'gross abnormality', as some members of the Presbyterian Church propose, pluralism equally requires that we permit abortion where a child suffers from a less serious handicap, or none at all. Since pluralism, in its true meaning, must allow for abortion on *any* ground which a person may happen conscientiously to support, it must openly admit that it extends to abortion on demand.

The logical pluralist solution to diversity of views on abortion is to legalise abortion on the basis that those who consider abortion to be right are free to have an abortion, while those who consider it wrong are free not to do so. If we apply this argument to another moral context we can perhaps see its structure more clearly. It would mean, for example, that the law should permit a man to rape a woman if he considered this to be morally acceptable. We surely would not accept that rape should be legalised to accommodate the man's conscience.

See also Fletcher, *A Protestant Minister's View,* in R. Hall ed., *Abortion in a Changing World,* vol. 1, at 25 (1970).

22. Cf. B. Nathanson & R. Ostling, *Aborting America,* Appendix B (1979). Reporting on the position of the various denominations in the United States, the authors state (at 300-302) that the Episcopal Church, after 1973, 'decided to oppose all legal restrictions, while speaking against abortions undertaken "lightly" or "for convenience".' The United Methodist Church in its 1972 *Social Principles* endorsed 'the legal option for abortion'. The United Church of Christ in its 1977 synod 'opposed efforts to negate the Supreme Court decisions or to limit public funding, and favoured forcing publicly aided hospitals to provide abortions, while protecting the right of conscience [f] or medical personnel.' The United Presbyterian Church, in its General Assembly resolution of 1972 endorsed 'full freedom of personal choice' in secular law.

23. Cf. B. Nathanson & R. Ostling, *supra,* at 295-298.

More generally we would object to a law which permitted a person to cause physical injury and pain to another merely because that person regarded this as morally justifiable.[24] No legal system in any country is based on such a broad principle of deference to diversity of moral viewpoints in a society. Why should the case of abortion be different?

A pluralist law on abortion offers the 'right to choose' abortion but it does so by denying the unborn the right to life. Some (but by no means all) of those who support this approach argue that they consider the unborn not to be 'really' or 'fully' human[25] and that on this account they should be free to terminate these less-than-fully-human lives. The pluralist thesis, it will be recalled, does not seek to argue that any particular attitude towards abortion is right or wrong: on the contrary it proposes that *every* attitude should be accommodated by the law. If, therefore, one person conscientiously denies that another is 'fully' human, the pluralist thesis requires that the law should not intervene if he or she terminates the life of that other person. The philosophical basis of this approach thus makes

24. This principle extends in law to cases of cruelty to animals: cf. *Duncan v. Pope,* 19 Cox 241 (1899).

25. Thus the Irish Women's Right to Choose Group write as follows:

"The anti-choice lobby argues that a foetus can be equalled with a person. But certain biological and social facts deny that this is so. An 8 week foetus is about the same as an adult's thumb nail. Shown a photograph of an 8 week foetus, it would be impossible for most of us to distinguish between a human and other mammal's foetus. A pig, rabbit and human foetus are almost identical at this stage of development.

"While in the womb the foetus cannot breathe and is totally dependent upon the maternal blood supply for oxygen and every component of its growth. It reacts to stimuli, but cannot feel pain as pain is a learned response, and the foetal brain is not developed enough to interpret the stimuli that it receives. Like all mammalian foetuses, it develops a heart beat, circulatory system and brain. But that doesn't make it a person.

'What is it we value about human life? No doubt you will think of important things like friendship and family ties, maybe the wonderful feeling people sometimes have, simply of being alive. You may think of various kinds of enjoyable and fulfilling experiences. But nobody can say that a foetus experiences the joys of friendship and human society. In a technical sense, a foetus is a human (as opposed to some other species) and it's living (as opposed to dead) — so in some sense there's human life in a pregnant woman's womb. But isn't it obvious that it has none of the things which we consider important or valuable about human life, that makes life worth living?

'We would never deny that a foetus is *potentially* a person, but this does not mean we should lose sight of the difference between our rights as women and the potential rights of the foetus. The humanity it has is abstract, and cannot be compared with that of the pregnant woman without devaluing her life, her needs and aspirations.' *Abortion: A Choice for Irish Women,* pp. 8-9.

the right to life of every person secondary to how another person perceives their human status.

THE AMENDMENT AND BEYOND

The amendment will have the effect of confirming the legal protection for the right to life of the unborn which most legal commentators hope — and some believe — the Constitution already affords the unborn. All that the amendment will do is to remove the nagging uncertainty on this question.

Of course, the amendment, being a matter of constitutional law, cannot itself resolve the social and economic pressures on women to have an abortion. But it is abundantly clear that, if our law asserts that we are pro-life in relation to the unborn, there is a very clear duty on our society through its laws and its social and economic policy to provide a positively caring and supportive environment for women. In practice this means that our law should completely remove the status of illegitimacy, as the Law Reform Commission have recommended.[26] The legal rights of all children should be made equal, irrespective of the marital status of their parents.[27] In the social and economic areas, the present financial support system for single mothers should be greatly extended and improved. In the area of housing, single mothers face formidable difficulties. While the local authorities do their utmost to operate the system of housing entitlements as equitably as possible, the stark reality is that there simply is not enough of the type of accommodation best suited to the needs of these families. In the private area, single parents face the difficulties that confront all parents with young children who are looking for rented accommodation; in some cases their position is worsened by a discrimatory attitude on the part of landlords. The needs in the area of housing are obvious. The position can be improved without delay if the political will is present. It is the obligation of all who support the constitutional protection of the life of the unborn to do their utmost — whatever the fate of the referendum — to give practical meaning to their commitment in these ways.

A final legal point may be mentioned. Some sincere people, while wholeheartedly supporting the view that the law should protect the unborn, nevertheless feel that legislation would be a more appro-

---

26. In its *Report on Illegitimacy* (LRC 4-1982).
27. The Law Reform Commission makes detailed proposals to this effect in its *Report on Illegitmacy*, supra, fn. 26.

priate means of providing this protection than a constitutional amendment.

This would, of course, be an understandable approach in a country where the Constitution merely declared specific rights and did not give a power to interpret or further extend those rights to the courts. But since we have a Constitution which confers a significant power on the courts to strike down legislation, there is — and can be — no guarantee that *any* legislation protecting the unborn would at present survive judicial scrutiny.

The forthcoming referendum gives the electorate the opportunity to ensure that the present doubt about the constitutional position of the unborn is removed. Those who support this step are, however, under the most serious obligation to do their utmost to bring pressure for change in a wide range of social and economic areas which have already been mentioned to try to remove the present pressures on women and to create a positively supportive environment for mothers and their children.

Text of Amendment Published

BERNARD TREACY, O.P.

The publication on 2 November 1982 of the proposed text of a constitutional amendment to protect the right to life of the unborn marks a new stage in the debate.

The proposal is to add to Article 40.3 of the Constitution, the article protecting fundamental rights including the right to life, the following sub-section:

3° The State acknowledges the right to life of the unborn and, with due regard to the equal right to life of the mother, guarantees by its laws to respect, and, as far as practicable, by its laws to defend and vindicate that right.

This formula is quite straightforward. It simply makes explicit in Article 40 what the Supreme Court had already held to be implicit therein. In two important cases (*G. v. An Bord Uchtala* and *Magee v. Attorney General*) judges of the Supreme Court had expressed the view that the constitutional protection of the right to life (Article 40.3.2°) extends to the unborn.[1] The formula of amendment does no more than make this doctrine an explicit part of the text of the Constitution.

In this amendment there is no attempt to hide the possibility of conflicts arising between the equal rights of the mother and child; and there is nothing here which would prevent a Court or the Oireachtas from providing for the resolution of those problems.

With this amendment one group of non-citizens, the unborn, will have their right to life explicitly protected in the Constitution. For all other non-citizens, however, problems remain, as has been argued on pages 76 and 77. Fundamental rights, including the right to life, are guaranteed in the text to citizens. This suggests that non-citizens enjoy no such protection. Not that there is any real problem at present, for natural law thinking is so dominant at present that the right to life of all human persons would certainly be upheld in the Superior Courts. But it would be altogether better that the text of the Constitution would explicitly guarantee the right to life to all human persons and not only to citizens.

1. Cf. pp. 74 and 75 *supra*.

Wording of the Proposed Amendment

CONLETH A. BYRNE, O.P.

The suggested wording of the proposed amendment (*supra*) does not differ significantly in its meaning from the wording I myself suggested (p. 65). Though repeating the legal formula '*respect, defend and vindicate*' sounds ponderous as a piece of English prose, it may be preferable as a piece of legal draftsmanship. Also, the equal right to life of the mother, implicit in my wording, as an instance of the general right to life of every citizen, is made explicit in the official wording. This is all to the good, to set some expressed worries at rest. Finally, the proposed wording avoids the pitfalls against which I suggested Fr O'Mahony was trying to warn the prospective drafters. Without containing anything of a confessional or sectarian nature, it seems to have managed to satisfy the aspirations of all those, in every confession and none, who wish to protect unborn life, in principle at least.

It will not satisfy those who see liberalized abortion as the solution to some of our problems. Neither will it stop abortion being resorted to, at home or abroad, to solve these Irish problems. A lot more needs to be done to change attitudes and social structures, before this will no longer be a problem here. Some people will doubtless think the money and energy expended to get this amendment through could have been better spent on making these other necessary changes. At least, let this not be the end of our expenditure of thought and effort and money on this issue. Otherwise we may justly be charged with insensitivity and hypocrisy.

Besides, the amendment as proposed may not be as effective in outlawing abortion here as some of its proponents would hope. To my mind, it attempts to avoid being divisive at the cost of a certain vagueness. For example, it does not clearly state at what point from fertilization to birth the unborn begin to enjoy this right to life, equal to that of the mother. Neither does it spell out clearly what is to be done in the case of a conflict of 'equal rights' between the unborn and its mother. Maybe it cannot do these things without running into the problems of confessionalism and divisiveness it seeks to avoid. Yet this very fact could lead in the future to the kind of court challenges to the law that the proponents of the amendment seem to be most anxious to avoid. The resulting judicial decisions could lead to either a tightening or a loosening of the law.

Still, I must leave these questions to professional lawyers and accept that maybe this is the best that can be done for now from a legal standpoint, leaving further developments to be dealt with as they arise.

This book is a *Doctrine and Life Special*

Forthcoming Titles in this series

Irish Neutrality and Nuclear Deterrence
Edited by Bill MacSweeney

Irish Values and Attitudes:
Irish Report on the European Values Study Group
Michael Fogarty, Liam Ryan, and Joseph Lee

Charismatic Renewal in Ireland: the Ecumenical Dimension
Virginia Kennerly
Preface by Robin Boyd

Report on Namibia
and
The Case against Immigration to South Africa
Banned Statements by the Bishops of South Africa